Reflections of a Fat Girl
Wisdom Lost and Found from Growing Up Overweight

Ilene Leshinsky

Copyright © 2020 Ilene Leshinsky

All rights reserved. No part of this book may be reproduced in any form or by any electronic or mechanical means, including information storage and retrieval systems, without permission in writing from the author or publisher, except by reviewers, who may quote brief passages in a review.

Printed in the United States of America.

Published by Altimese Nichole Enterprise, LLC

Book Design by Darío de los Santos

Book Formatting by Darío de los Santos

ISBN 978-1-7324115-6-2

The information provided in this book is designed to provide helpful information on the subjects discussed. This book is not meant to be used, nor should it be used, to diagnose or treat any medical condition. For diagnosis or treatment of any medical problem, consult your own physician. The publisher and author are not responsible for any specific health or allergy needs that may require medical supervision and are not liable for any damages or negative consequences from any treatment, action, application or preparation, to any person reading or following the information in this book. References are provided for informational purposes only and do not constitute endorsement of any websites or other sources. Readers should be aware that the websites listed in this book may change.

To learn more about Find Body Freedom or its Founder, Ilene Leshinsky, MSW, visit www.findbodyfreedom.com.

Contents

Introduction	7
Chapter 1: Body Acceptance, Positivity – And Yes, Body Love!	13
Chapter 2: Are You Hungry? For What?	51
Chapter 3: You Can't Fool Body Wisdom… So, Why Not Follow Yours?	79
Chapter 4: It's Not Selfish… It's Self-love!	105
Chapter 5: More Reflections… on Culture, Society, Men, and Aging	129
Conclusion	163

Introduction

In the beginning...

Yes, I was a fat girl!

I was 6 lbs., 9 oz. when I was born, at normal weight, so I'm told. But by the time I was five years old, I was fat, actually, very fat!

Usually, I take issue with anyone using the word "fat". In this culture, it's not simply a descriptive word, such as short or tall. It's often used as a "four-letter" word, with hidden – and not so hidden – messages of bias, disdain, and disgust. However, I deliberately use the word "FAT" because it describes most accurately how I felt growing up. You'll hear all about that in the article titled "My Story".

Reflections of a Fat Girl is a book of articles that I wrote from 2009 to 2016. I was a psychotherapist in private practice, working primarily with women who were grappling with the stuff of women's lives - depression, anxiety, past and present traumas, relationship challenges, and oftentimes issues with body image, weight, and eating. They came to me because they wanted more joy and fulfillment in their lives.

Every month during that time, I wrote a column for *Jill*, a women's magazine, which was published by the local newspaper, the Press-Republican, in Plattsburgh, NY. I loved writing the articles. And if truth be told – I loved seeing my writings in print.

If you're a woman, I think you'll find that this book speaks to you. And if you're not, you'll find it enlightening and full of lessons about how women struggle with their bodies.

Why the title? Well, since for so much of my life, I hated my body, or was running away from my body, or desperately trying to change my body, all because I was fat or believed I was fat, the articles reflect that. And the articles reflect my coming to terms with my body as I learned about the immense wisdom it holds.

Ilene Leshinsky

The articles are about everything and anything that has to do with women. Using my own life, the women I worked with in therapy, local happenings, national or cultural events, songs, movies, or even "discussions" with my husband, I wrote and wrote and wrote about what it's like to be a woman in this culture, at a time when we have more power and control over our lives than ever before – and less diversity of "acceptable" body types than ever before.

You'll recognize yourself in many of the articles. And because I share with you how I learned to be more loving and compassionate with myself, I believe that you will learn from them, as the articles are loaded with information, tips, tools, strategies, research, and data.

What's important for you to know is that almost everything I have done professionally over the last twenty-five years has been a way for me to come to terms with growing up fat – including my articles for *Jill*. So, you'll experience the articles sprinkled with compassion for any of us women who have felt judged or been shamed for our body size and shape.

You'll also hear some anger toward a culture that still expects us to look—and behave—a certain way in order to be loved and accepted.

You'll also read a lot about some of my clients – anonymously, of course - who worked hard to free themselves from the fantasies of body perfection.

At the time I wrote for *Jill*, BodySense was the name of my program for women. To clarify, it is now called Find Body Freedom. The rebranding was a result of my focus on the importance of positive body image for women – and for men.

The book is divided into five chapters for easy reading. You can read the chapters in the order they appear or find a title that jumps out at you.

ENJOY!

My Story

I wrote this article in January of 2012 when I was a monthly contributor to a woman's magazine (Jill) in Plattsburgh, NY. It's as true today as it was then. What you see in italics are new thoughts and feelings about My Story, as my evolution continues to unfold.

When I was a very little girl, the story goes: I didn't eat very much. This made my mother anxious. In those days, babies were supposed to be plump, with dimpled arms and thighs. So with prompting from my grandmother who lived through famine and displacement in the Old Country, my mom found "creative" ways to get me to eat what they considered "enough". One strategy she used was dancing around the kitchen with a mop on her head. When I laughed, she shoveled a spoonful of food in my mouth. Great plan to ease my mother's anxieties. However, intuitive eating proponents would argue, not a great way to support the innate wisdom of the body – my body.

By age five, I was very overweight and was shamed by family and friends for my weight, size, and eating behaviors. ("Do you really need that second helping, Ilene?") And I was put on diet pills in the fourth grade. My mother shared with me, many years later, that she used to watch me walk down the street on my way home to lunch while sneaking a candy bar from my pocket into my mouth. Every day, it seemed, I would stop by the corner variety store for a sweet treat BEFORE coming home for lunch! So, surprise, surprise, I developed into a sneak eater by the time I was ten years old.

In adolescence, I was depressed and anxious. By the time I was a young adult, I was lost, lonely, and looking for love in all the wrong places. And, I was swinging from the extremes of compulsive overeating to highly restrictive eating on a regular basis. For those two decades, I struggled with diets, my weight, and with my urges and cravings. I was driven by the socio-cultural messages to be thin – *really* thin – without regard for what my body was trying to tell me. It took many, many years for me to undo the harm that was done to me, and that I did to myself.

Ilene Leshinsky

This is the part of my story where I tell you how a graham cracker changed my life. Yes, a graham cracker! And it's the part of the story where I tell you that in my early thirties, I joined Weight Watchers. Because I was so lost and finally realized that I could not do "this" alone – this stuff of eating like a normal person – I became a WW member, leader, and trainer. I loved Weight Watchers for the sense of community it provided and because the program introduced me to vegetables, a missing food group in my life.

Long story short, I was leading a meeting on a Wednesday night in Brookline, MA, with ninety women looking at me like I held the answers to the never-before disclosed mystery of weight loss and maintenance. And I had *just* binged. And as I'm listening to their questions, a voice in my head is saying, "Ilene, you are such a fraud and a hypocrite. You just binged!"

So, promise you won't laugh when I tell you about the binge. Before coming to the meeting, I ate four graham crackers. Not four boxes! Not four sleeves of crackers! Four graham crackers! But in those days, the WW serving size for grahams was three – and I had just eaten *four*. And, to me, because I was, and in some ways still am, a rule-follower, that one extra cracker constituted a binge.

I know, I know. How ridiculous! But here's the part where I experienced an epiphany, the big "aha" As one voice is yelling at me, another voice is asking, "Why are you letting any person or program tell you what to eat and how much to eat? You hold that knowledge and wisdom. YOU, Ilene, are the expert about your body!" And it was at that moment of confusion and then complete clarity that Find Body Freedom was born. (*I have rebranded the program from The Gateway Group to BodySense and now to Find Body Freedom.*) And it was also that moment that planted the seed for me to go back to school for a Master of Social Work degree and to become a psychotherapist.

So, as you can see, one graham cracker changed my life!

This transformation was both a physical and psychological undertaking. Physically, I had to learn that my body sends me signals that I am hungry. What a concept! My body gets hungry and lets me know that it needs refueling. I also had to learn that when I am hungry, there are certain categories of foods that make me feel energized (those high in proteins, good fats, and complex carbs) and those that make my stomach cramp (high-sugar foods) or make me want to take a nap (foods high in not-so-good fat).

Becoming attuned to my body's hunger rhythms felt both empowering and scary. Psychologically, I struggled. I went back and forth from "eating is good" (it fuels both the brain and body, and boy, did I feel a difference) to "eating is bad" (it may cause weight gain and no one will love me if I weigh a few more pounds).

As I learned, little by little, to trust my body, I had to contend with the flood of so many hurtful and abusive memories of being a "fat kid". I didn't recognize until I was in my late twenties and thirties (and in my own therapy) how I had been scarred by the intentional or unintentional comments from parents, family, and friends about the size and shape of my body. But I didn't know that then. Statements, looks, and eye rolls were a regular part of my life.

There were no programs or groups at that time for those of us wanting to break the diet/ binge cycle, although there were a growing number of women writing about attuned or intuitive eating or demand feeding (among them Geneen Roth, Carol Munter, Jane Hirschmann, Susan Kano, Judith Matz, and Linda Bacon). It was a lonely journey for me, but ultimately a highly rewarding one that led me to creating the original program, The Gateway Group, in 1992. The greatest gift that those visionary women gave me and that I gave to myself was freedom – freedom from food, weight, and body image obsessions, as well as freedom to enjoy food appropriately. I say "appropriately" because I am a now mindful eater. I eat when I'm hungry and I stop when my body, not my mind, tells me I've had enough.

Like me, most of my clients say that the easiest part of intuitive eating is learning about their hunger. The toughest part, however, is determining when enough is enough. I remember grappling with the following questions as if they were the mysteries of the universe: Should I eat everything on my plate just because it's there? What do I do if I'm still hungry (true body hunger!) after I've eaten the "serving size" of a particular food? I'm not hungry now, but I'm scared—will I get hungry in the middle of a staff meeting or on a three-hour car trip?

With much trial and error, as it is with most things in life, I let my body lead me to a place of knowing when I was hungry and when I had had enough. And this was quite the feat for me! For those of us who have felt emotionally deprived in our lives, when we've felt that we have never gotten "enough" or that no amount of anything could fill us up, this intersection between the physical and the emotional can be tricky. Hence the trial and error and the importance of paying attention during the eating process, experiencing how every bite of food changes our awareness of filling our bellies.

So, now food has become fuel for my body and brain—tasty fuel, but fuel nonetheless. It is no longer my best friend. It is no longer a means to assuage my emotional wounds. When I stopped eating emotionally and stopped starving or stuffing myself into oblivion, I was able to identify the areas of my life in need of an emotional makeover.

These are just some of the areas with which I struggled, and on some days, still do (can you relate?): If I'm not thin/skinny, will someone love me? How do I stop all the negative thoughts about my body that I've been saying to myself for my whole life? How do I stop comparing my body to the bodies of other women? Can I forgive the people in my life who wounded me with their intended or unintended comments about my body?

So, the little girl who didn't eat enough for her mom and the woman who ate way too much or way too little for all the wrong reasons found her way to health and well-being (both physically and emotionally) by letting her body lead the way.

It's my story... and I'm sticking to it! By the way, it can be your story, too.

Chapter 1:
Body Acceptance, Positivity – And Yes, Body Love!

When I was nine years old, I remember my mother calling me inside to take a phone call from "a boy", she excitedly said. I had been playing outside with friends on a brisk and bright autumn afternoon.

My mother handed me the receiver from the wall phone (does anyone reading this remember those?) and saying "Hello" with the same level of anticipation as my mother.

The voice on the other end, young and male, said, "You're fat!" And the phone call ended. He had hung up. I can still feel the sting of shame that I felt on that day. I hung up the phone and walked out of the house without looking at my mom and without responding to her questions.

That was one of many memorable body image wounds that I experienced as a young child. That one and the others left their imprints, their scars. Years ago, their memories threw me into a tailspin of shame and anger. Today, I can remember them like one remembers scenes from a movie that are experienced from a distance.

Over the years, decades actually, I have worked daily to love my body and it has rewarded me with health, well-being, and lots of energy and vitality. My body and I are partners in life!

The articles in this chapter express the challenges of women to love the bodies we're in. And by the way, the work is worth it!

Ilene Leshinsky

I Love My Body!

Did you know that the majority of women and girls in this country feel negatively about their bodies? Did you know that these negative feelings often lead to increased depression, anxiety, and life-threatening eating disorders? I didn't need Thomas F. Cash and Linda Smolak who edited "Body Image, A Handbook of Science, Practice, and Prevention" to tell me this. I lived it – for over half of my life.

And now, I love my body. Yes, I love my body with all of its curves and creaks, its bumps and its imperfections. And no, I didn't swallow a magic pill or undergo brain surgery to feel this way. My love and appreciation of my body is the result of years of focused work on self-care and seeing my body as not just an ornament, or a pretty or sexy object, but as a vehicle by which I move through my life, achieve my goals, and have happy, healthy relationships. Cash and Smolak would agree. Women, according to the research, become increasingly satisfied with their bodies as they age, particularly between the ages of 60 and 85. But you don't have to have your Medicare card or collect Social Security benefits to feel positively about your body.

What we know – and what the literature tells us over and over – is that body image messages are powerfully transmitted by the media, by family, and by peers and more often than not the messages are negative, unrealistic, and designed to make us feel bad about ourselves. One of my clients was so distressed that her six year old daughter, tall for her age and slender, cried in the bathtub, "Mommy, I'm fat!" Does she hear girls talking about their bodies at school? Maybe. Does mom make comments about her daughter's body or her eating habits? No, she tells me. Has mom ever made negative comments about her own body in front of her daughter? Yes!

And then we must look at the great and powerful mass media – television, movies, and magazines – in which images of the sociocultural beauty ideal in women have become increasingly thinner over recent decades. Cash and Smolak cite, "One analysis of Miss America pageant winners and Playboy centerfolds documented a significant decrease in body size from the 1950's to the 1990's, by which time the majority had weights that were more than 15% below their expected weight for height." And to further compound the problem, they say that levels of thinness have continued to drop but with the added pressure of needing at least a medium size bust and toned muscles, in addition to being tall and thin. Did you know that the average fashion model has a Body Mass Index of 16.3, well below the normal range of 18.4 – 24.9? And that these models now weigh 23% less that the average woman? So every time we turn on TV, go to the movies, or open a magazine we see images of who we are not!

So what's a woman to do? I loved reading the research because it reinforced my own beliefs and highlighted my own evolution. As women, mothers, transmitters of powerful messages ourselves, we need to challenge (even just in our own minds) the current, narrow, and for the majority of us, impossible to achieve standard of beauty. Information is power! And having the knowledge that we are seeing unhealthy messages and images is helpful. It certainly was helpful to me to deconstruct my faulty belief system about beauty.

Cash and Smolak identify two other compensatory factors that have been shown to offset negative body image. Firstly, women and girls who move their bodies through sports or regular exercise have more positive feelings about their bodies than females who don't. In my own life I know this to be true. When I started to experience exercise as a way to achieve long-term health and well-being, rather than short-term weight loss, I saw (and see) my body as powerful and strong – and yes, as attractive.

The second factor is intuitive eating. Sound familiar? If you've been reading my articles for a while, you'll recognize that intuitive eating, the idea that we are all born knowing how to eat healthily is at the core of BodySense. How validating for me and for those of us who eat from this approach, to know that body appreciation and intuitive eating are strongly linked.

Ilene Leshinsky

And on a personal note, as I've gotten older, I've come to realize that my body is my home. And I love being home!

What I Wish My Mother Had Said to Me...

In an ideal world, our mothers had the insight and the emotional wherewithal to guide us on the often tumultuous seas of our development. This is particularly important when we girls start to notice that we are different from them, from others in our world, and from the culture at large.

A client sent me this letter from a mother to her daughter. The mom of three young girls is Cathy Cassini Adams, a blogger, licensed clinical social worker, an elementary school teacher, and a yoga instructor. This letter to her daughter, about self-love, struck a chord with my client and with me. I share excerpts with you in hopes that it will start a dialogue between you and your daughters and with the other special women in your life.

"Lately you have been asking about your body – wondering about your size and shape, why you look the way you do, why others look different. Important questions that I'm glad you asked, and for now, this is my answer:

You were born to be you.

You are not supposed to look like your sister, like me or like any of your classmates. You might notice similarities, and that's fine, but you are completely unique. You are important to this world, you are supposed to be here, and the design of your body is part of the greater plan of who you are – it should be no other way.

You may hear that you are supposed to look like this or that, or you may notice magazines or billboards that reflect a certain image, but they aren't real. They are people, just like you, who have been made up, and airbrushed. This isn't reality, it's their work.

It's great to have a healthy body and feel good about how you look, but self love is not about falling in love with your appearance. It's about knowing your insides – your bliss, your gifts, your ability to share and experience joy.

Ilene Leshinsky

Self love will hold you up in every aspect of your life because people will treat you as you treat yourself. When you love yourself you won't allow others to take advantage of you...

Taking care of yourself is your most important job – it's the only way you will have energy to take care of others. So don't waste time disliking yourself, spend time noticing your beauty instead. If you do, you will notice that everybody is beautiful and you will be surrounded by people and experiences that reflect this understanding...

So it's your job to have faith in that [inside] place, to remember that it's not outside, it's not another person, it's not in your clothes, it's not in a job, and it's not in a grade or an award.

It's only in you.

And only you can celebrate the outside and the inside of being you; so make it a celebration to remember.

And when you forget, please come back and ask. I am here to remind you."

And says Ilene, when YOU forget, dear Jill reader (and you probably will), I am here to remind you!

Cathy can be found at www.cathycadams.com or www.zenparentingradio.com.

Body Image Insights from an Aging Goddess

March is my birthday month. As you are reading this I am now 42 years old. Okay, I'm using the new math – that 60 is the new 40. On every birthday, I take time to reflect on my life. Am I happy with my work? Yes! Am I happy in my marriage? Yes! Do I like getting older? Yes… and no. It's challenging at best to be "women of a particular age" in a youth and size 2 obsessed culture. More often than not, when I look in the mirror I like what I see – a woman who has laugh lines and compassion written on her face and a body that is strong and healthy, although sprinkled with signs of aging. So most of the time I like myself. And I even like the way I look.

However, when was the last time any of us saw ourselves reflected in a commercial, print ad, movie, or television program unless depicted as a mother, grandmother, or woman in need of a weight loss product or surgery? Have you noticed that some of the diet ads show women who we would give our eye teeth to look at, like thinking it is time to start a diet? I challenge you to find a commercial for a cruise line or a restaurant where the average American woman – 5'4" tall, 140 lbs, and size 14 - is represented. Sociologists say that if we do not see ourselves represented in the culture at large we become invisible, feel "less than", and find our self-esteem plummeting. Many of my clients bemoan (and berate) their physical selves because they cannot find themselves when they open a magazine or turn on the TV.

The reality is we are not going to change the world of advertising. The fashion business and the $33 billion dollar diet industry are too powerful for that. However, we can challenge the cultural norms, each of us in our own way. Beauty – real beauty – comes in all shapes, sizes, and colors. Have you seen the Dove Soap campaign at www.realbeauty.com? It's worth checking out and sharing with the younger women and girls in your life. It debunks many beauty myths and promotes self-esteem and self-worth from the inside out. If we, adult women, don't challenge those superficial, cultural messages ourselves, we subtly and not so subtly send those same messages to our daughters about their value based on their size and weight only. Just look as these alarming statistics:

~80% of ten year old girls are worried about becoming fat

~ 80% of girls in the fourth grade are on diets

~ 40% of first through third grade girls want to be thinner

If we don't transform the way we think about our physical selves we are condemning another generation of women to lives of weight, size, and eating obsessions. (FYI... the prevalence of anorexia nervosa has increased by 30% every five years since the 1950's.)

Let's face it! Our bodies are constantly changing – through puberty, childbirth, menopause, and as we become aging Goddesses. So let's stop selling ourselves short. Let's celebrate who we are, the quality of our character, our many accomplishments. Let's work toward better health and well being for ourselves and for all women. Let's look in the mirror and like what we see – women of integrity and of fine character, women who are multi-talented, kind, and generous.

Happy Birthday to me and to all March Goddesses!

Get a Ph.D. in Body Image!

I'm getting a Phd.! According to Dr. Christiane Northrup, any woman who looks at her naked body in a full-length mirror, every day, is in a Body Image Ph.D. program. You may have seen Dr. Northrup during Mountain Lake PBS fundraisers and she's written several books including "Women's Bodies, Women's Wisdom" and "The Wisdom of Menopause". She's an OB-GYN and dispenser of important wisdom to women regarding our physical and mental health. I love her spirit and her energy.

Dr. Northrup suggests (and I would agree) that we learn to love our bodies. The first step is by taking care of them – fueling them with healthy foods, exercising them regularly, resting them when they need sleep. She also recommends that we look at them, clothed and unclothed, and often. How else can we learn about them and notice their changes? This resistance that we women have to looking at our bodies, particularly our naked bodies, keeps many of us from self-exams for breast health and skin checks for melanomas.

When I ask my clients to embark on this journey, some roll their eyes, some laugh hysterically, and some cry. "Ilene, I haven't looked at myself from the neck down in years", is often what I hear. Believe me, I understand firsthand the courage it takes to look at a body that does not conform to the cultural ideal and that we have ignored for years. My clients tell me that looking in the mirror brings up shame, disgust, fear, a lifetime of negative self-judgments. I know! And we need to look anyway! If we do, a transformation process takes place. Over time, the more we look at our bodies, the more we appreciate them. The more we appreciate them, the more we like them (maybe even love them). And the more we look, the more gentle our eyes become.

One of my clients brought to session the February edition of Glamour Magazine because there was a six-page fashion spread she wanted me to see. The title was "You can look even better naked" and the photos depicted model Crystal Renn in nude colored garments from lingerie to evening dresses. Crystal Renn is gorgeous! And she's a size 12 (considered "plus-size" by the industry standards and "average-size" by us American women). My client was so excited to see a representation of her own body type in Glamour. "Look!" she said, "I recognize my thighs and my arms and my cleavage!" To Glamour's credit, nowhere in the spread was there mention of a "plus-size" anything.

What my client didn't know was that Crystal Renn has written a book entitled "Hungry: A Young Model's Story of Appetite, Ambition and the Ultimate Embrace of Curves" in which she explores her journey from chubby cheerleader, to top model, first as a depressed and ultra-thin size 2, and then to a voluptuous and healthy size 12. She addresses her decision, as she watched her hair fall out, her deadening eyes, and graying skin, to eat – to eat so that she could experience the joys of life and of the fashion industry that she loves. She also wrote the book, she says, to change the way everyone perceives beauty.

As we see more Crystal Renn's in magazines, on television, and on the big screen, maybe it will become easier for us to look at our own bodies – to accept them, take care of them, and yes, to love them, at whatever size. And maybe someday we'll even think we're beautiful! But we can't wait for the fashion industry to catch up. So why not join me right now. Begin your own Body Image Ph. D. program. Every day, look at yourself in a full-length mirror. If you do, someday you'll be standing there naked!

"The Great Body Acceptance Debate"

I will never be a runway model. At five feet, I'm too short and as an Aging Goddess, I'm too old. Being height and size challenged for much of my life, body acceptance has been an on-going challenge for me.

When I was in my early thirties and very, very thin, a man I was seeing told me that I had the body of a twelve year old. I automatically heard the remark as a compliment. It didn't dawn on me until many years later that he might have been commenting on how unwomanly I looked, without breasts and hips. Women (and this woman) have been struggling with the issue of size and weight acceptance for what seems to be forever.

This spring's fashion week in New York and in Europe prompted a great deal of discussion about just these issues. Are designers who make their samples in size zero or double zero (do you believe it?) unwittingly promoting eating disorders in young and not so young women? An article in the New York Post by fashion editor Robin Givhan explained that since fashion layouts are photographed months before the designs appear in magazines and in stores, the only clothes available are the samples - and only a "profoundly skinny woman" (a quote from Givhan) can wear them. So when you and I flip through a fashion magazine, we're interpreting what we see as what we "should" look like – as the ideal of beauty. We're also getting the message that thin is healthy.

Walking down the runway this year were also "plus-size" models. Givhan addresses the issue that many of my clients bring to me. How can the fashion industry call these size 12 models plus-size when the average American woman is a size 14? And what am I – "super-size"? They are asking good questions - and from that - other ones according to Givhan (and Leshinsky). "(W)hen does plus-size, in a profoundly overweight population, become just as distressingly unhealthy an image as emaciation?" How does a culture celebrate beauty in all shapes and sizes even when the statistics are letting us know that certain sizes are unhealthy?

Are certain sizes unhealthy? These are weighty questions. (Pun intended!) And let's not forget the hidden population of unhealthy size 2's that are easily overlooked in the face of society's judgmental feelings about size 22's.

I have been promoting body acceptance for decades – but not at the expense of good health! We women need to take a deep breath and then take stock of ourselves. We need to ask: More often than not, am I following sound nutritional guidelines for eating? Am I exercising three to five times a week, for thirty minutes? Am I sleeping an average of eight hours per night? Are my blood pressure, cholesterol, glucose, electrolyte and potassium numbers within normal range? Some of the above can be answered by an honest appraisal of what we do and don't do. Some, however, can only be answered in consultation with a physician. When was the last time we had an annual exam, including blood work?

I love this quote from Givhan: "Somewhere between emaciation and obesity lies good health. And somewhere between those extremes there is also a definition of beauty that is inclusive, sound, and honest". So on our way to healthy, we might just look in the mirror one day and see a vibrant, beautiful woman staring back at us, at whatever size we're in!

We Owe It To Our Daughters

When I was a little girl and my mother didn't want my family to know what she was saying, she spoke in French. I have memories of her and my aunts looking at me, and laughingly saying "grosse fesse". For my non-French Canadian readers, it loosely translates to "fat ass".

In recent studies of eating disordered college students, the participants were asked to trace the sources of their eating issues and obsessive body focus. The vast majority shared that along with the cultural pressure to be thin, their eating and body disturbances began with a negative comment by a family member, authority figure or peer when they were children. Fast-forward to my adolescence. I'm on the beach on a hot summer day, in long pants and one of my father's oxford shirts, having lost 45 pounds during my first year at college, and telling a male friend that yes, although had I lost many sizes and pounds, I still had a "fat ass".

In my family, appearance was a high priority. My mother was a beautiful woman who went to the hair salon weekly and shopped in high-end boutiques. She and my not so fashionable father would subtly and not to subtly comment on the size and shape of relatives, friends, and strangers. I learned very early that thin, attractive women hold power. But, I was short and fat, although with such a pretty face.

When I first sit with my adolescent and young adult clients, I ask them when they first became aware of their focus on controlling their food intake and their bodies. Most of them state that they heard negative remarks about their eating and/or their bodies from family members. The vast majority grew up with mothers who have or had their own struggles with feeling loved and accepted in the bodies they're in.

Am I blaming those mothers? Am I blaming us? Absolutely not! We, too, grew up in a culture that promotes "body beautiful" at any cost.

Ilene Leshinsky

However, it's time for us to examine our own beliefs about our bodies, and how we communicate those to our daughters (and sons). Are we expecting the multi-billion diet industry to promote body acceptance and intuitive eating? Don't hold your breath, dear readers! Only we can change the cultural landscape by changing the attitudes we hold, and the words we choose when talking to ourselves and to our daughters.

During my mammogram last year, the tech and I struck up a conversation about body image. Her thirteen year old daughter had shown her a picture of a model in a fashion magazine and said "I'm fat. I need to go on a diet". Mom, the woman making my right breast into a pancake, took her daughter to the computer and gave her a lesson in airbrushing and photoshop. Her daughter, referring to the picture of the model, exclaimed, "She's not real. She's fake!" I don't remember your name, Mom, but you're my hero and a role model for us all!

The Skinny on Fat

May 21, 2012 was "Fat Day" on The View. The television show's co-hosts, Barbara Walters, Joy Behar, and Elizabeth Hasselbeck, scheduled a series of experts to explore our country's epidemic rise of obesity and Type II Diabetes. Queen of comfort food, Paula Deen, sitting in for Whoopi Goldberg, and Sherri Shepherd were the guest co-hosts. Deen was recently diagnosed with diabetes and has just lost thirty pounds.

It seems to me that FAT has become a four-letter word in this country and I wondered how many people would change the channel or turn off the TV, missing the important information from the experts, rather than being insulted by the show's title. Elizabeth was the only co-host concerned about the name of the program. So was I.

I have issues with the word fat, both professionally and personally. Many of my clients sit with me and say "I'm fat", using the word as a negative descriptor of all they are, as if one word sums up everything about them, as if they have absorbed all of our culture's negative stereotypes. To them, fat equals stupid, slovenly, unkempt, out of control, unlovable, unprofessional, unhireable. Some of these women are a size 2 and some are a size 22.

When I was in the fifth grade, I remember playing outside my house and hearing the phone ring. My mother excitedly called me inside to take the call, mouthing to me, "It's a boy". I took the receiver (remember those?) from her and said hello. The unidentified male voice on the other end laughingly said, "You're fat", and quickly hung up. It's been five decades since that moment, and I can still feel the shame. Yes, I have issues with the word fat.

A few weeks ago, after reading an article in the Press-Republican titled, "No end to US obesity epidemic in sight", my husband turned to me and said, "Ilene, you're in a growth industry". (No pun intended.) So what happened in this country that has led to the prediction, according to this article, that by 2030, forty percent of

Ilene Leshinsky

US Adults will be obese and that severe obesity will double, when eleven percent of adults will be nearly 100 pounds overweight? Easy access to highly processed foods? Bad parenting? Fewer and fewer gym classes in our schools? Family dinners at fast food drive-throughs? Too much TV watching? Too much time on the computer? Too little outside play? School lunches loaded with fat? Restaurants that give us double or triple the amount of food we need to fuel our bodies? The list could go on and on if we're looking for something or someone to blame.

And, according to Dr. Oz, who was one of the experts on The View, since I personally experienced childhood obesity, I had an eighty-five percent chance of becoming an obese adult. But I'm not an obese adult. I finally took responsibility for what and how much food I put in my mouth - and why. I finally learned that diets don't work and that according to the National Eating Disorders Association (NEDA), dieters gain back their weight within one to five years. Extreme exercise doesn't work either, as a long term approach to weight loss and management. What does work? Fueling our bodies with nutritious foods when we are hungry (not angry or sad or lonely or even joyous), stopping when our bellies are full (not stuffed), and moving our bodies regularly. Simple? Yes. Easy? No!

We are a culture of extremes. We glorify thinness as the ideal of beauty, on one hand, and are repulsed by obesity on the other. Seventy-eight million Americans are obese (article) while ten million females and one million males in this country have an eating disorder (NEDA), in part as a result of our national obsession with thin/ skinny.

What often gets lost in the "fat debate" is that these young and not so young women and men are engaged in life-threatening behaviors. Yes, people die as a consequence of obesity. And sadly, many people also die from anorexia and bulimia as well. But where is the public outrage at industries and a whole culture that glorifies a "look" that is unattainable for the vast majority, and keeps girls and boys, women and men focused on external beauty? When did we start confusing thin with healthy and beauty with skinny?

Proud to Be a Tortoise!

Remember the Aesop's fable "The Tortoise and the Hare"? It's the story of a lightning-fast rabbit and a plod-along turtle that are seemingly mismatched in a race. It was the tortoise, annoyed with the hare's boastful assertions of being faster than the wind, that challenged the hare. To the surprise of everyone but the tortoise, (s)he wins. Well I'm a tortoise. For most of my life, I've put one foot in front of the other, to get to the finish line, to achieve my goals. "Slow and steady wins the race"!

The other morning, as I was doing my usual jog around the Oval, a very young woman ran past me – no, she blew past me. For a moment, I watched my competitive self pick up speed to catch her, until a voice in my head asked "Why?". I quickly did some self-talk and reminded myself of the reasons I run in the first place – not to win a race, but for the long-term benefits of health and well being.

In a society that promotes quick fixes, instant cures, weight loss overnight, flat abs in two weeks (I could go on and on and on), it's hard to be a tortoise. It's hard to believe that there is value in putting one foot in front of the other daily. It's challenging at best to keep the faith that the small steps we take will get us to our goals, no matter what they are.

The night before my last birthday, I couldn't sleep. So not to wake my husband, I went downstairs, turned on the television, and started flipping through the channels. Within an hour I had written down phone numbers for products and services promising me flawless skin in seconds, thin thighs in two weeks, reduction of belly fat (without surgery or changing my eating habits!) and a free consultation with a former IRS agent who would assist me in reducing or eliminating my 2009 taxes. I picked up the phone a few times, but didn't dial. Common sense prevailed.

It's so difficult not to get sucked into the "quick fix" mentality that pervades our culture. We've listened to our friends and colleagues at lunch or around the water cooler excitedly talk about the newest diet, program, or exercise craze. They (and we) want "it" and we want it now. And then so often, a few weeks or months later we hear (or experience ourselves) "it didn't work". Did "it" not work? Or like the hare in the fable, did we not work it, consistently putting forth the effort, putting one foot in front of the other, one day at a time.

I've been following **BodySense** guidelines for over two decades and exercising regularly for three. Perfectly? Absolutely not! Consistently? Absolutely yes! I eat from hunger (true body hunger) and I stop eating when my body (not my mind) has had enough. My former selves, the sneak-eating child, the bingeing adolescent, and the young woman who restricted her food intake to near starvation, well, they have become a woman, this woman, with a healthy and stable relationship with food, and a loving, appreciation for her body.

When we shift our focus from quick fixes and instant cures to living each day mindfully, eating nutritiously, exercising regularly, putting one proverbial foot in front of the other, we wake up one day and realize: I am a tortoise and I am proud!

Bellies and Buttocks and Breasts, Oh My!

Remember in the Wizard of Oz when Dorothy, the scarecrow, the tin man, and the lion were walking through the forest with arms linked, afraid of lions and tigers and bears? Are we women fearful that our bodies will burst forth with womanly parts like Dorothy and her companions were scared of the wild animals lurking behind trees and bushes? Where did they go? Where are they – our bellies and buttocks and breasts?

I became an adolescent on the cusp between Marilyn Monroe and Twiggy. Size 12 Marilyn, curvaceous and sexy, and 91 pound Twiggy, fab, fashionable and with an androgynous body. Talk about a radical shift in the beauty ideal! One minute (or so it seemed) the culture was glorifying female flesh (remember the paintings of Rubens, Titian, and Renoir?) and the next minute preadolescent bodies were the rage. What happened?

Some sociologists and feminist writers have theorized that as women have gained more power, as we use our voices, as we demand more equality, as women get bigger, so to speak, our bodies have gotten smaller. They point to 1920 when women won the right to vote and the subsequent decade of flapper bodies that were lean and angular and to the feminist movement of the 1960's when "mod bods" were the fashion ideal, while women were challenging gender roles and stereotypes.

Regardless of theories, it's hard to start a business, be a political leader, write a book, run a household, when we're starving ourselves. It's hard to have a creative or coherent thought when we wake up in the morning obsessed with food and go to bed each night hungry. I sit with women of all ages and sizes who are consumed with thoughts of food and hatred of their bodies. This cycle keeps them (us) trapped.

Don't you find it interesting that as a society we have become so much more accepting of so many things – racial, ethnic, and religious differences, sexual orientation, interracial unions? But when it comes to beauty and body size we have a fixed and very limited idea of what is acceptable? Do you see yourself when you open a magazine, turn on the TV, or go to the movies? Unless you're a size 2 or less, you don't. And as a result, and without our knowing what happened, most of us become marginalized and invisible. If I don't see myself in the culture at large, do I even exist?

In 1960, the Twilight Zone aired an episode entitled "Eye of the Beholder" in which a woman underwent eleven surgeries in order to make herself "fit in". When her facial bandages are removed, we see a beautiful young woman with perfect features by our standards but we see disappointment and horror on the faces of the doctors and nurses. When the camera focuses on them we realize that they are deformed, by our standards with heavy brows and pig-like snouts, but the epitome of beauty by theirs. Have we become that society where only thin is beautiful and fat is ugly, where there are only two places to land on the body size continuum – fat or thin?

There are some bright spots on the cultural landscape, however. There are larger models whose bodies are reminiscent of Marilyn's. And there are some television shows, such as Ugly Betty, Drop Dead Diva, and even Grey's Anatomy, in which a few of the female leads are larger women – with bellies and buttocks and breasts – who are smart and sexy. Remember the movie "Real Women Have Curves"? We also see Dove products showing women of all shapes and sizes in their skin care commercials.

However, can we wait for the media and the diet industry to give us permission to love our natural shapes and sizes, our womanly parts? I don't think so! And besides, that's our job anyway.

For Better or for Worse…It's Summer Time!

On a beautiful Saturday in May I facilitated my second "Boost Your Body Image" workshop. Eight amazing women participated, ranging in age from nineteen to sixty-five. All of them with body image issues and all of them unhappily anticipating this coming summer season with tank tops, sleeveless sundresses, shorts of varying lengths… **and the dreaded bathing suit.**

Interestingly, around the same time, another one of my clients, also with body image issues and very thin, was telling me about her mid-winter vacation in Jamaica. She is on her beach chair, in her one piece bathing suit and a cover up and she's watching two larger women (probably not American, she says) walk by her in bikinis. And she couldn't help but notice that numerous men were following these women with their eyes as they sashayed down the beach, exuding sensuality and sex appeal. By our cultural standards of beauty, she says, these women were "fat". By theirs, they appeared comfortable in their bodies, enjoying the beach – and turning heads.

When talking about their bodies, my workshop participants laugh – and cry – about their bat-winged underarm flesh, their flabby knees, and their bulbous bellies. Who would want to see all this in a bathing suit, they ask?

I get it! I really do! Whether at an extra-large or an extra-small, I did not want to be seen in a bathing suit or even shorts for that matter. There's so much pressure on us women in this culture to participate in a summer activity – such as swimming in a lake or simply walking around the Oval – while looking good (or sexy and toned) with whitened teeth, sleek, shiny hair, and creamy skin (without acne or age spots). How do we muster the courage to go out of the house in the morning? How do we find the time for our exercise, diet, and beauty regimens?

Or… we simply decide to live our lives in the bodies we're in!

Remember seeing pictures of women at the beach "in the olden days", in the early 1900's, dressed in bathing suits with long sleeves and pantaloons down to their knees? Are we longing for those "good ole days", to be covered up, to feel less exposed because we don't have "perfect" bodies? In 2013, we are blessed with so many freedoms that our "foremothers" didn't have – and couldn't even imagine. Yet what remains the same for many of us (for most of us?) is the focus on body beautiful that traps us, and as we discussed on that Saturday morning in May, shrinks our lives.

I have this fantasy that we women are at the beach (it's my fantasy so we're at the ocean). Hundreds of us - in all shapes and sizes and all heights and colors - are waiting for the sun to rise. And when the first glimmers of golden orange peak over the water, in our brightly colored bathing suits (no blacks or browns for us!) we dance into the water with wild abandon and greet the day as the Sun Goddesses that we truly are.

In my fantasy, we live in a culture where we women are comfortable in our bodies, where they bring us joy, where we take great pleasure in eating healthy foods that make our bodies sing, where we feel passionate about our partners and feel sensual when we make love. We're the only ones who can transform the culture. We're the only ones who can transform the way we see ourselves and the way we feel about this home we call our bodies.

And maybe it starts with buying a bright red bathing suit!

Reflections of a Fat Girl

Body Image – Self Image

A hundred years ago, Renoir painted "La Toilette" (The Bather), a portrait of a young woman in the nude. She has long, auburn hair, full breasts and hips, a rounded belly, and, if the truth be told, thighs that look like mine. She's voluptuous and she's beautiful! One hundred years ago she was the ideal of feminine beauty. Today, she'd be one of my clients, struggling to accept herself in the face of an unattainable beauty ideal. When I show her to my clients, some of them are heartened by the resemblance they see to themselves. Some think she has such a pretty face, but boy is she fat.

Today, the average Supermodel is 5'11" tall, weighs 117 lbs. and wears a size 2. The average Supermom is 5'4" tall, 140 lbs. and is a size 14.

What happened? What changed in a hundred years for women? I could wax philosophical on the sociopolitical changes that women have faced in the past one hundred years. I could explore the profusion of media images we receive daily, that subtly and not so subtly, tell us that we are not acceptable the way we are. I could share with you the many untold stories of women living with eating disorders, in a futile attempt to attain today's standard of female beauty. But I won't. (That should be a Women's Studies course at Plattsburgh State.)

What I will say, however, is that approximately 80% of women (and girls) in this country don't like their bodies and as a result don't like themselves a whole lot. 40% of first, second, and third grade girls want to be thinner. And 90% of high school girls think they are overweight. Not only are we obsessed, so are our daughters.

Million, billion dollar industries have been created tapping into our insecurities. Our thighs are too thick, our stomachs too round, our underarms too jiggly, our breasts too small or too saggy. For every flaw, for every imperfection, there's a product or a program to fix us. Perfect body equals perfect life. Right? Wrong! What we really want is to feel good about ourselves, to feel acceptable to ourselves, and to see ourselves reflected in the images we see in magazines and on the big and little screen.

I'm a therapist so I'm a firm believer in self-improvement, both physical and emotional. However, I'm not a believer in self-flagellation. I'm also not a believer in a culture that makes 80% of us (probably an underestimate) feel inadequate. I am, though, a believer that we women (and our male counterparts) need to be strong and healthy. We need to exercise regularly, eat nutritious foods, get eight hours of sleep a night, and spend quality time with the people (and animals) in our lives who make us smile. And we need to appreciate ourselves for who we are, for all that we do and that includes having gratitude for the bodies we are blessed with. Yes, you heard me, blessed! Our bodies perform the myriad of tasks we ask them to do every day. They lift, they bend, they stretch, they walk, they run, so that we can do the jobs of our lives. Yet instead of thanking them, we berate them for being too short, too fat, too round, too bumpy, too this, too that. How about a little gratitude!

How do we reconcile the bodies we have with the body we want? We can start with gratitude. Every day, as I'm getting out of the bath or shower, I look at my naked body in the mirror and say "Thank you. Thank you for all that you do for me. Thank you for the joy of walking my dog and wrapping my arms around my husband." The point is that these are the bodies we have. We can spend our lives belittling them or we can learn to love and appreciate them right now – as they are – and watch them change as we take better care of ourselves. It's a choice, your choice. Which one will you make?

Body Acceptance: What We Can Learn from Men

I think that men have it easier than women. No, I'm not going to discuss the state of the feminist movement in 2009, nor the equal pay for equal work debate. However, I am going to state that men have more body acceptance than women – and we women can learn a lot about this from men.

Surprise, surprise! There is a distinct difference in the way men and women view their bodies. Men see their bodies as functional – what their bodies can do, the tasks they can perform. We women see our bodies as ornamental – how attractive we look and to what degree our bodies conform to the cultural ideal of beauty. Men focus on function. Women focus on form. In general, men don't see themselves as fat until their body size gets in the way of something they want to do. As we know, we women think we're fat if we don't measure up to the media images with which we are bombarded daily. Seeing ourselves as ornaments, it's hard not to feel inadequate.

"I hate my body", I hear so many women say. That's a strong and powerful statement. Often it translates into "I hate myself. I'm not acceptable. I'm not lovable." There is often a profound sense of despair that envelops us when we compare our bodies with those of other women. We compare, we criticize, and we come up short. Oh, to be free of those body image comparisons and expectations! (Have you noticed that we hear more about the shape of First Lady, Michelle Obama's arms than we do about her Harvard Law degree?)

Also, our lives get smaller. They begin to shrink when we feel our own bodies are unacceptable. Here's a little quiz. See if you answer yes to any of the following:

- I avoid parties or other social situations because of my body size.

- I have not applied for a new job because I'm afraid I will be judged by my size rather than my abilities.

- I don't wear shorts or sleeveless tops in the summer even though I get uncomfortable in the heat.

- I don't go swimming because I don't want to be seen in a bathing suit.

- I don't have sex as often as my partner would like because I don't want my body seen or touched.

This list could go on and on and I'm sure you could add to it.

So how can we feel better about our bodies? How can we develop body acceptance? We can start by learning a lesson from the men in our lives. (Don't tell my husband that I just said that.) We can focus on function rather than just on form. Everything we do should be in service of becoming stronger and healthier – in mind, body, and spirit. (Perchance, if we become more attractive as a byproduct of those efforts, well then, that's icing on the proverbial cake!)

When we eat, are our food choices promoting strong bones and sharp minds? Are we getting enough sleep to restore our bodies and brains? Or do we abuse our bodies with inadequate amounts of nutrition and not enough restorative sleep? And... speaking of function, bodies were made to move. Regular exercise builds healthy bones, turns fat into muscle, and sends endorphins coursing through our brains. (By the way, there is something very attractive about a well-fed, well-rested, vibrantly healthy woman!)

So let's make this vow together:

I do hereby declare that from this day forward I will choose to accept my body in its natural size and shape. I will celebrate all that my body can do for me each and every day. I will treat my body with respect, giving it enough rest, refueling it with nutritious food, exercising it regularly, listening to what it needs, and responding accordingly. I will choose to resist our society's pressures to judge myself and others based on body weight, shape, or size. I will believe that my self-esteem and identity come from within. And I will affirm that I am worthy and lovable, right now, exactly as I am! (From the National Association of Eating Disorder "Declaration of Independence")

"When Women Stop Hating Their Bodies"

Go get a piece of paper and a pen, right now, please. And do a little exercise with me. Without any editing, write down all of the negative thoughts you had about your body yesterday. That's right, all of them! Your list might include: I'm fat. I feel fat. My belly is huge. My thighs jiggle. My upper arms keep waving long after my hand has stopped. I'm the biggest woman in the room. My body is ugly. My breasts hang down to my knees.

Does the above list look anything like yours? Do your thoughts repeat and repeat and repeat during the course of the day? How do these thoughts make you feel? Energized? Ready to tackle the world? Or depleted, defeated, drained of energy? My guess is the latter.

Okay, now for part two of this nonscientific experiment. Estimate how many minutes or hours of yesterday you spent thinking these thoughts. Five minutes? Five hours? I think you would agree that if we spent only five seconds belittling ourselves and our bodies, well, that would be too much. If only a few of us women experienced these thoughts, then we wouldn't have what many theorists consider an epidemic of body hatred. Believe it or not, these negative thoughts are experienced by women of all shapes and sizes and of all ages. Lean women and round ones, eleven year olds and women in their sixties and beyond have similar thoughts.

In their 1995 ground breaking book "When Women Stop Hating Their Bodies", co-authors Carol Munter and Jane Hirschmann explore what they term "bad body fever", the proliferation of negative thoughts that women have about their bodies, most of the time. They ask us to examine the price we pay physically and psychologically for entertaining these thoughts. They also ask us to look at what these thoughts really mean.

Get this. They speculate that bad body thoughts, the negative thoughts that we have about our bodies, are never about our bodies, and always about our lives! When we have a not so nice thought about our bodies, what are we really saying? So reread your list and try to "decode" what your thoughts really mean.

When we say, "I feel fat", right before an important job interview, are we really saying we're nervous about not fitting in? When we think, "My belly's so big and disgusting", are we really saying that our lives are too full, too overextended and there's no time left over for us? When we say "My upper arms are fat", are we bemoaning having too many burdens to carry? Right now, some of you are thinking that translating bad body thoughts makes sense. Others, well not so much. You're shaking your heads insisting that you are indeed fat and your belly is truly big and disgusting. But if we're honest with ourselves, we know we had these same thoughts when we were bigger – and when we were smaller.

So – just maybe, the problem is not with our bodies, but with our lives! Maybe if we're scrupulously honest with ourselves, we'll acknowledge that parts of our lives need fixing, rather than parts of our bodies. Maybe my relationship with my partner is not as loving as it used to be. Maybe I'm worried sick that my child or spouse is drinking too much. Maybe my job is unsatisfying and I'm no longer valued for my skills and talents. The list could go on and on of some significant life issues that are causing us distress and possibly increased caloric intake.

So what do we do? Do we eat restrictively, exercise excessively, undergo surgeries to feel better about the stuff of our lives that have absolutely nothing to with the shape and size of our bodies? Or do we tackle our life issues?

Yes, we need to eat healthily and yes, we need to move our bodies to maintain health and well-being. However, I am suggesting that we get real with ourselves (did I just sound like Dr. Phil?) and put our energies where they belong – into fixing our lives and accepting our bodies.

"There is Beauty in the World..."
And It Comes in All Shapes and Sizes

A couple of things happened this past August that made me wonder about beauty and what it means to be beautiful.

At the beginning of the month, I went to a fancy schmancy family wedding in Newport, Rhode Island. There were people there I had not seen in decades. (That's what happens when you move to the North Country!) It was a bit unsettling at first as some people remarked how I looked the same and others, how different I looked from the last time we had seen each other. Some knew me as smaller and some as larger. I watched myself reflected in their eyes, and after a few deep breaths, I was okay.

The band was fabulous, with a great brass section so my husband and I danced the night away. Since I'm a pretty good multi-tasker, I watched the wedding guests move their bodies, while I was moving mine. From very young to very old, people were out on the dance floor having a blast. Short bodies, tall bodies, round ones and lean, we were all groovin' to the music. It was beautiful to watch. And if some were self-conscious about their size, weight, or shape, I couldn't tell.

You put a bunch of families in the same room and you find similarities and anomalies. One branch of my family is tall and lean. Another one, the one I'm from, tends toward shorter and rounder. (And then there's my younger sister who is nine inches taller than I am!) All of us were decked out in our evening attire - and beautiful.

Also in August, we adopted a dog from the Adirondack Humane Society. Our Sophie died in January of this year and I have been so missing doggie love and kisses. So after more than a few visits to the shelter, Roxie is now a part of our family.

What struck me during the selection process was the wide variety of breeds, mixed breeds, shapes, sizes, and weights of the residents. One might say a microcosm of the dog world – and of our own. Now I can't know for sure, but I don't think any of the dogs, including Roxie, have low self-esteem because of her/ his weight, size, or shape. And… I'm pretty sure that many dogs have been adopted over the years that do not look like supermodels.

The point? We can be so accepting that beauty comes in all shapes and sizes in the natural world, in animals, plants, trees, and shrubs. But oh how difficult it is for us to accept that our bodies – women's bodies – come in all shapes and sizes – and are beautiful!

I know this is so hard. I know this is such a challenge. But can we stop comparing ourselves to other women? Can we stop fantasizing that their lives are better, happier than ours because their thighs are thinner or their abs are flatter? Let's put the focus where it belongs – for each of us – on creating a life worth living. And in that life we are strong, healthy, creative and wonderful women. We take as good care of ourselves as we do the others in our lives. And because of that, we are beautiful!

As the song by Macy Gray goes, "There is beauty in the world. So much beauty in the world. Always beauty in the world. So much beauty in the world." We are part of that beauty. We come in all shapes and sizes. And yes, we are beautiful!

Reflections of a Fat Girl

Loving the Skin that You're In – at Any Age

I say this to so many of my clients: Women's bodies are designed to change – from childhood into puberty (remember the onset of breasts and hips?), in pregnancy, in menopause, and through our senior years. I've been saying this for years so you might think that the concept has sunk into this woman's head! So at sixty-five and a half, why am I surprised that my body is still changing? Did I think that I was immune to the passage of time, to metabolic changes, and to the effects of the aging process?

I remember the exact moment I looked into the mirror and saw my mother's face staring back at me and no, it wasn't a hallucination. I was surprised – okay, shocked – to see the same landscape of lines, wrinkles, and creases on my face as I remember my mother having when she was getting older. Did I think that just because I've been using moisturizer since age fifteen that my face wouldn't tell time?

And my body... how did this avid exerciser and clean and mindful eater get a rounded belly, a thicker middle, and crinkly skin on her inner thighs and upper arms?

As I'm grappling with these deeply existential questions (just kidding), I see a video on the Today Show. Women of different races and ethnicities, in their 60's, 70's, and 80's were grooving to music and addressing how blessed they feel to be alive and in the bodies they're in. Some were taller and thinner, some shorter and rounder – and all of them with the footprints of time on their faces and bodies. And, they were beautiful – and so grateful for their many joys and strengthened by their inevitable losses! All of them with the wisdom that only the aging process can bring.

In the same Today Show segment, Roz Warren, a humor columnist for the New York Times, was interviewed about her recent story "At Ease with a Body Fighting Gravity". She's almost 60 she says and not the "looker" she used to be in her teens and twenties. Back then, she wore geeky glasses and didn't have a clue why male heads turned when she walked by. She quips that if her 16 year old self, who was highly critical of every one of her physical flaws, saw her almost 60 year old body, she'd scream, "Shoot me now!" Roz also shares the story of trying on bathing suits in the dressing room of a sporting goods store with her significant other watching. She invited him in as there was nowhere for him to sit and wait for her. It made his day, she says, and hers – both of them enjoying the experience of watching her 58 year old body wiggle in and out of spandex.

Roz reminded me of my own trip into bravery, the last time I bought bathing suits and modeled all three for my husband. I made his day, too – although, I confess, I put them on and took them off in the bathroom. (Okay, so I'm not as secure as Roz or maybe as you, dear reader, thought I was.)

Would it have been different for me – my feelings about my body as I've aged – if I had spent childhood and adolescence as a thin person? Maybe. Does it matter now? Probably not. I've sat with so many women who tell me they were "normal" kids in "normal size" bodies. And now they too are grappling with the aging process. And I've also sat with women, who like Roz Warren, say they were real "lookers" in their youths, bodies and faces that could turn heads. They describe the sadness they felt when it – the ability to turn heads – stopped happening. Even Eleanor Roosevelt, one of my personal heroes, when asked towards the end of her life what she wanted and didn't have, said that she always wished she'd been prettier. Wow!

So maybe, aging is the great equalizer. We all do it. There's no way around it (unless of course we are willing to spend all of our time, energy, and disposable income on diet programs, plastic surgeries, Botox injections, tummy tucks, liposuction, and the latest and greatest exercise craze.) So maybe it's time to start celebrating that we're alive – at whatever age – healthy, or on our way there – honoring our inner beauty and seeing how our outer self is transformed by loving ourselves for who we are, rather than what we look like. And this shift, I truly believe, will lead us all to loving the skin that we're in – at any age.

"Mirror, Mirror on the Wall"

This summer, I did one of the most courageous things a woman can do – I tried on bathing suits – and actually purchased two! We were going on vacation in August, renting a house for a week on the Atlantic and I wanted to go to the beach in a bathing suit that flattered my body type and felt comfortable. The last time I bought a swimsuit was about six years ago when I walked into Sam's Club, pulled a $15.00 Speedo tankini off the rack and brought it home. The pattern was cute, but the cut, well, not so comfortable. In those six years, I'd worn it twice.

So this year, I bit the proverbial bullet and ordered seven designer suits from a high end retailer that was having a 50-65% off swimsuit sale, figuring that one of them would fit and I could try them on in the privacy of my home. Well, to my surprise and dismay, I didn't like even one of them.

Still undeterred, because I was on a mission, I went to our local TJ Maxx. After fifteen tries, I found two that worked with my body type. It was interesting to pull up a once-piece, loaded with spandex, and watch my belly and breasts move north. (Why aren't bathing suits made with zippers?) The whole experience was a lesson in self and body acceptance and an opportunity to practice what I preach to my clients.

In the story "Snow White and the Seven Dwarfs", the evil queen asks over and over, "Mirror, mirror on the wall, who in the land is fairest of all?" And every time she hears from the mirror, "You, my queen, are the fairest of all" – until one day Snow White's image appears. There's a lesson in this fairytale for all of us.

If we're solely focused on our external selves – how pretty we are, how thin, how toned, if we're worried about not being loved, accepted, or desired because our abs aren't flat enough or our hips and bellies are too big, we'll see other women around us (our sisters) as the enemy, as competition. We'll worry, that in comparison, we won't measure up. Why? Because there will always be someone else who looks better to us – if we come from that place of judgment, of self and others.

However, if we daily (or sometimes moment to moment) challenge the notion that there is only one ideal of beauty, then when we look in the mirror we can see a beautiful self shining through, one that is uniquely us, one that is a combination of genetic factors and a commitment to good self-care. I have promoted this for years and have seen it come to fruition in my own life and in my experience with the mirror. When I eat when I'm hungry (eating nutritious foods that fuel my body) and stop when my body has had enough (yes, you can do this too!) and when I exercise regularly, I like what I see in the mirror. Reflected back to me is glowing, vibrant, good health! Even as we age, if we respect our bodies by taking good care of them, we like (okay, accept) what we see in the mirror. Our bodies reward us for our attention with radiant, physical and mental health.

In addition to consistent self-care, affirmations have been so helpful on my journey to body and self-acceptance. Here are a few that I worked for me:

~ I am loveable exactly as I am.

~ I treat my body with respect, fueling it, moving it, and resting it appropriately.

~ I appreciate my body for all that it has done for me.

And try this. As you're drying off after your shower or bath, talk to your body parts in a loving, gentle way, with gratitude. "Thank you, legs, for moving me through my day." "Thank you, belly, for digesting my food." "Thank you, arms, for carrying my burdens." Appreciation for what our bodies do, not just how they look, goes a long way toward self-acceptance.

So… "Mirror, mirror on the wall, who in the land is fairest of all?" I am – and so are you!

If I'm Not Skinny, Does that Mean I'm Fat?

I've spent a lot of time over the years thinking about my body. Not if it's healthy I'm ashamed to say, but if it's attractive, sexy, or toned. And most of the time, I've been disappointed with my self-assessment. How about you?

If you go online to look at female body types, you'll see some sites showing two types (the apple and the pear), some claiming women come in six varieties, and some others saying we fall into one of twelve categories. As best as I can figure, I'm a pear, or a short cello, or a bumpy (my adjective) hourglass. Anyway, does it matter? Maybe if I'm buying jeans it's helpful to know that I shouldn't try on a style for women or girls with narrow hips. What also has been helpful though, is learning that women come in so many shapes and sizes. If we're watching TV or going to the movies or flipping through magazines, that reality can get lost on us.

I've also noticed that we live in a dichotomous world where things, ideas, or people are portrayed as good or bad, black or white, Republican or Democrat, or thin or fat. What about those of us who do not fall on either end of the social, political, or size/weight continuum? Can we be okay with being in the middle? Can we be okay with who we are or what we look like if we are or are not a size 2? Can we just be okay with who we are?

I ponder these questions. If I'm not skinny (and at a size 8 petite, I'm not) does that mean I'm fat? And by whose standards? If I'm comparing myself to a Victoria Secrets model, well maybe. Maybe not if I look at the nudes painted by Rubens, Titian, or Renoir. I sit with women and girls who are smaller than I, who with sadness and sometimes hatred in their voices and on their faces exclaim, "I'm fat". And I sit with women and girls who feel like they don't fit into today's society – and don't deserve to take space in the world because they are not a size 2 or 12.

It seems to me that for hundreds of years women have been struggling with fitting in – into our prescribed roles or into our lives in the bodies we were designed to have. Late 1800 advertisements in circulars and magazines depict women buying bustles and corsets to plump up their derrieres, hips, and bust lines. Now most ads in the popular media hype just the opposite. So... if we're hoping for validation from how our bodies look, some of us are always going to lose and some of us are always going to win?

So what's the solution? The article "Why 'Fat Talk' is Bad for Reaching Weight Loss Goals" on the website Real Age, Live Life to Your Youngest, makes the argument that negative body image talk ("I'm so fat." "My butt is so big." "Just look at my thunder thighs".) exacerbates our negative feelings about our bodies and actually leads to higher levels of depression and more pressure to be thin.

We all could benefit from the following tips from Camilla Mager, a clinical psychologist in New York City:

~ Avoid reading magazines that reinforce the body image problem.

~ Pay attention to your tone of voice when talking to or about yourself and your body.

~ Focus on what your body is capable of, your body's strengths, not its deficits.

~ Commit to NOT engaging in fat talk conversations with friends.

And... let's take really good care of ourselves by getting enough sleep, eating nutritious, fuel foods, exercising or moving regularly, and socializing as often as possible with friends and loved ones. And... let's practice a whole lot of self-acceptance!

Prime Time Women

I take an exercise class at the Wellness Center called Strong Bones. I love it. I love knowing that each set of exercises is strengthening my bones and muscles and supporting my core. And as much as I love moving my body, I love the women in the class. (I hope some of you are reading this.)

We range in age from our late 50's and early 60's into our 80's, although I think there is at least one outlier in her 40's. So yes, this class is designed for women in their prime.

Before class and during the cardio segments, you'll see us walking around the periphery of the gym, at different speeds, chatting with friends or simply moving our bodies. But once class begins, we're serious exercisers, using hand weights, exercise balls, and steps – strengthening our bodies, while focusing on balance and form.

We're all beautiful, all of us in the class, with our different body types and varying degrees of gray in our hair, and lines on our faces. We're all beautiful!

I wish I could reach back in time and tell my younger self, the self who struggled with healthy eating and body image issues in her teens, 20's, and 30's, that we're all beautiful. That it's not so much about how one looks, it's not about having the body type that's in vogue at the moment (at 5 feet tall and rounder than leaner, I was never "in style"), it's about being healthy and feeling good about one's self and about one's life. And when we do, when we feel good about ourselves and our lives, we exude this energy, this spirit, this vibrancy, that transforms us into beautiful. I believe that many women in my class know this.

My body type is certainly not the "body du jour", the long lean type that looks athletic. I'm short – and according to my last measurement at my doctor's office, getting shorter. And, I'm curvy. And I don't look good in spandex! I'm one of many body types in my exercise class. There are so many types. One website I've read says 2, another 13, and yet another 26. You'd never know that trying to buy fashionable clothes, including exercise clothes, that are only designed for the long and the lean. (Thank you, Melissa McCarthy for a clothing line for women with curves!)

Some of the women in my class are like me – short and rounder, but some are shorter and slender. Some are very tall. (I grew up with a younger sister who was 5'9" to my 5' so I've always longed for height). Some of us are shaped like apples, some like pears, and some like a goblet, a cello, an hourglass. I promise you that I don't look at us with judgment! I just love observing our differences, our uniqueness, and the beauty that is each of us.

These women in "extended middle age" (as defined by Jo Ann Jenkins, CEO for AARP) have made a commitment to taking care of themselves. Some, like me, are still working. Some volunteer. Some have commitments to family. All of us though take an hour of our day to get or stay strong and healthy. It's hot in that gym in summer where our class is held. But there we are, at least 25 of us, making our bones and bodies stronger.

My younger self would be shocked that I'm okay with more weight on my body, with a rounder belly, and with a more and more detailed road map on my face. But my younger self never experienced the freedom that aging brings – the freedom to appreciate the woman I have become, the freedom to be me, without the shackles of body image issues.

The research data states that women feel better about themselves and their bodies as they get older. Women with the best body image, the literature says, are those of us 60 and over. I see the same faces show up for class week after week to take care of themselves and to connect with each other. I'm guessing they feel the same way. We're Prime Time Women!

Chapter 2:
Are You Hungry? For What?

Thoughts on Eating – Intuitive, Compulsive, Restrictive, and Emotional

In my teens, my twenties, and most of my thirties, I ate as if I had no realization that there was a connection between hunger and health, between feeding myself and having energy, and no conception that my eating behaviors were very unhealthy. I was oblivious or in denial – or both.

I overate or underate, starved myself or binged. I ate when I was hungry – and often when I wasn't. To say the least, I had a conflictual relationship with food.

I remember one afternoon, sitting in my sister's kitchen and telling the sad tale of how a new man in my life unceremoniously broke up with me – with no warning and no reasons. I was devastated, and while telling her the tale, I ate an entire two-layered bin of Royal Dansk Danish All Butter Cookies. And… I remember not even feeling the least bit full.

So, this chapter is on all the ways we feed ourselves; what to do when we realize that we are not feeding body hunger, that we are not fueling our bodies; what to do when we begin to recognize that we are trying to calm and soothe our emotional wounds by eating – or, for many of us, not eating!

This chapter explores the different ways we use food and eating, ultimately what works and what does not, and how loving ourselves in these challenges is the only way through them!

Ilene Leshinsky

Hunger: Friend or Foe?

According to the countless weight management commercials and advertisements that we see on television and in print, hunger is our enemy. Hunger has to be controlled, managed, ignored, or tamed. And feeding our hunger will set off a cycle of frenzied, non stop eating. Right? Wrong!

Before I explore why the above notions are wrong, let me share that we women have gotten a bum wrap. We have been brainwashed to believe that hunger is bad, that if we give in to hunger we will not be able to stop eating. We have believed the messages of the $109 million dollar diet industry that we cannot find health and well being without the help of a diet. We have believed the messages of the fashion industry – that we are not acceptable, desirable, worthy of love, unless we are a size 0, or 2, or 4, or maybe we're okay at a size 8. (Think about the underlying message of this – in order to be a "something" we have to diet down to a "nothing" – a size 0.) We have been duped!

Some theorists who have explored this country's growing problem with weight have said that women in particular have dieted their way into obesity. Have you heard this expression, for every action there is an equal and opposite reaction? What this means to us women (paraphrasing Geneen Roth, an international weight management expert) is that, for every diet there is an equal and opposite binge. Deprivation triggers excess eating.

But I'm not here to point out what most of us already know... that diets don't work. I'm here to present an alternative approach to weight management, to health and well being, something that we can live with for life. Some people call it Feeding on Demand. Some call it Intuitive Eating. I call it Body Sense. And feeding our hunger is part of that sense or wisdom that each of our bodies has.

It's simple and the complete opposite of what we have come to believe. Hunger is natural, normal, and a sign of health. Hunger is a signal that the body needs refueling. Without feeding our bodies on a regular basis we can wreak havoc on our entire physical and mental system. Would we expect the car to go if the fuel gauge read empty? Of course not! However, we do expect our bodies to do their work and our brains to think clearly without proper nourishment. (And by the way, hot fudge sundaes and chocolate chip cookies do not constitute appropriate fuel for the body and brain. Sorry about that.) We need to learn to feed our hunger.

So how do we make the shift from controlling our hunger to trusting it? If we can hold the belief (and I know this is challenging) that our bodies have this innate wisdom (and they do), they will lead us to three simple (but not necessarily easy) principles. They are: Eat whatever you want (keeping healthy nutrition in mind); But eat only when you're hungry (true physical hunger, not cravings, urges, not from boredom, sadness or anxiety, and by the way, we can learn to manage these); And stop when you are comfortable, not stuffed.

Although what I'm going to say next is not directly related to hunger, it is an important principle in achieving health and well being. We need to regularly put movement into our lives. (Exercise is a "four letter word" for some people, so I've chosen to use the word movement.) Our bodies were made to move. If they weren't we wouldn't have arms and legs. We'd just be giant heads.

So we have a choice. We can continue to have an adversarial relationship with our bodies, to do battle with them, to treat our hunger as a dangerous, wild beast. Or... we can befriend our bodies, learn from their innate wisdom. We can experience hunger as natural and healthy. The first approach keeps us at war. The latter brings us peace, harmony, and health. Which one will you choose?

Ilene Leshinsky

Don't Pull the Trigger!

So did you make your list? Your list of triggers? Last month I asked us to explore the emotions, situations, and foods that propel us down the path to unconscious, mindless eating. Regardless of what they are, how long-standing and deep-seated, we no longer have to respond to our discomfort by eating when we are not hungry. What a novel idea! I have control over what I put in my mouth and when I do it!

Let me share one of my recent success stories. A month ago, my husband and I discovered a lump on our youngest cat, Mickey. And the lump was big! Where did it come from, we asked, as Mickey is always demanding attention and wanting to be rubbed down daily. After an examination by our veterinarian, Mickey went in for surgery on a Friday morning. My husband, who was going to pick him up later in the day, called me and left a voicemail message but the message was vague regarding what our vet found.

You know when you know that something is wrong by what someone says – or in this case – by what someone doesn't say? At that moment my anxiety started to rise and I found myself flying around my office looking for something – anything – to eat, to calm my nerves. An apple? A piece of hard candy? A can of soup? None of these would do the trick until I found the jar of peanut butter. As I opened the jar and started to shove the spoon into it, a voice inside me asked, "What are you doing, Ilene? Are you even hungry? Is mindlessly eating peanut butter going to change Mickey's prognosis?" So I closed the jar, sat down in my chair, and took a series of deep and cleansing breaths.

So what happened here? I paid attention – firstly to my rising anxiety. Secondly to the body wisdom that asked me to question my hunger level. And thirdly to the voice asking me to challenge the belief that my eating when I wasn't hungry would change the course of human (or cat) events.

And finally, I breathed. I cannot stress enough the importance of breathing – deep inhale breaths through the nose, and long, cleansing exhalations through the mouth. Breathing slows things down – the chatter or frenzy in our minds, our accelerated heart rates. And breathing fosters peace, calm, and the sense of balance that we need to make good decisions. In the moment of breath, we move from an adrenaline state where we are fired up, to the oxytocin state of well-being.

What I did not do in the above scenario was judge myself. It would have been easy for me, the **BodySense** expert, to yell at myself for even thinking of food to calm and soothe, let alone sitting with an open jar of peanut butter. If I had been self-punishing, I would have missed out on the awareness of another trigger situation – feeling completely out of control of the well-being of one of my loved ones.

Mickey is fine and healing well. I still have an unfinished jar of peanut butter in my office. Life is good!

Ilene Leshinsky

So If Diets Don't Work, What Does?

The very next day after I submitted last month's Jill article, in which I complained about feeling like a lone salmon, swimming in a sea of diet messages, trying to convey the innate wisdom of the body, I received my monthly issue of **Psychotherapy Networker.** The cover read **Diets and Our Demons. Does Anything Really Work?** To my delight, the whole magazine was filled with research-based articles about, eating, dieting, body image, and how our struggles with our lives often get played out in our relationship with food. Suddenly I felt like I was swimming with a sisterhood of salmon.

"The most frequently cited statistic (regarding the effectiveness of diets) according to Judith Matz, LCSW, in her article **Recipe for Life**, "is that 95 percent of dieters will regain the lost pounds". Personally and collectively, we know the truth of this. How many diets have we tried – and failed? How much money have we spent on frozen foods, supplements, books, programs, memberships, and equipment that promise to change our bodies, only to find that weeks, months, or a few years later, we're right back where we started. And then we feel bad about ourselves. We interpret our "failure" as lack of will power or self-control. Yet again we have failed to follow the plan. Yet again our bodies have betrayed us. What we do not realize is that we have waged a battle between mind and body. Our minds are telling us that this diet will give us the body we want. But our bodies are fighting the intentional decrease of calories with an increase in the desire to eat.

According to Matz (and I agree), diets "promote a loss of internal signals for hunger and fullness that are necessary for normal eating". When we deny hunger, when we don't feed our bodies enough, we negate their innate wisdom of when to eat and what to eat. "There's growing evidence", says Matz, "that diets make us fat!"

Another compelling argument is that genetics plays a major role in determining our size and shape. (Some research states 40%.) Matz says that studies show that the weight of adopted children more closely resembles that of their biological parents than their adoptive ones. Other research indicates that when identical twins were raised separately, their body mass index was nearly identical, supporting the influence of genetic inheritance, rather than environment. Even metabolism plays a role in determining our weight. Resting metabolism accounts for 70% of the calories we burn and according to some of the recent literature, about 40-80% of resting metabolism may be inherited.

So if diets don't work (and possibly can make us fatter), what does? The "attuned" or "intuitive" eating movement started in the 1980's with proponents such as Geneen Roth (Breaking Free from Compulsive Eating), Susie Orbach (Fat is a Feminist Issue) and Carol Munter and Jane Hirschman (Overcoming Overeating and When Women Stop Hating Their Bodies) telling us that even after decades of dieting we could relearn how to eat in a normal way, following our natural hunger and satiety rhythms. We were born knowing how to eat, they told us in the 80's and many researchers are saying the same thing today.

But every time we ignore hunger, every time we become shaky, weak, irritable, light-headed, we have waited too long to eat. And you know we do this – with the idea that if we skip this meal and maybe the next, we'll reduce our caloric intake, lose weight, and achieve the body we see splashed across the media. Unfortunately, what actually happens is we throw our bodies into metabolic crisis and we end up eating more as a result. And every time this happens we find it more and more difficult to accept ourselves in the bodies we're in. How sad! And to paraphrase Dr. Phil, is this workin' for us?

Ilene Leshinsky

The Day I Ate the Whole Thing

Well actually, there were many days throughout my life that I ate the whole thing. A whole half gallon of chocolate chip ice cream along with an entire Sarah Lee All Butter Chocolate Cake, on one occasion. Two huge chocolate chip cookies, a giant bag of Doritos, and a two liter bottle of Tab, on another. Two oversized tacos with two sides of onion rings and French fries, on yet another. Back in the day I didn't drink or do drugs to transport my brain and body to another place. I ate... and ate... and ate. And it didn't matter if I was larger or smaller.

I have always loved the taste of foods loaded with fat and sugar. I'm wired that way. And I'm especially drawn to foods that combine sweet and salty tastes. The right combination of sugar and salt sends my brain to dopamine heaven. But then the aftermath, the food hangover, the bloated belly and the guilt and the shame in the wake of a binge. (Know what I mean?)

I'm a mindful eater now. Not perfect, but mindful. I actually practice what I teach, being in the present moment while eating, chewing my food before swallowing it, putting my eating utensil down between bites. As a result, surprise, surprise, I eat less. And I don't require as much food to satisfy me as I used to.

But before you think I'm the paragon of eating virtue, let me tell you about the time in recent history that I ate the whole thing – or almost the whole thing. It was the weekend before we – my husband, dog, and I – were scheduled to drive to Florida for our two-week serotonin boosting vacation. Busy doesn't come close to describing the activity in our household. Scheduling clients before and after our trip, holding the newspaper and mail deliveries, organizing dog food and medicines, packing, unpacking, and packing (too much) again. Instructions for our cat sitter and getting the car ready for the long distance transporting of our large dog. You get the picture. All those little details that can make or break an experience.

Reflections of a Fat Girl

So it's Sunday at around noontime, after breakfast, and before tackling all of the aforementioned tasks. I'm sitting at the kitchen counter, reading the Sunday Press-Republican. I look down and find myself almost at the bottom of a bag of potato chips – salt and vinegar, my favorite. Granted, the bag was only a two serving size but it's not the quantity as much as the mindlessness of the behavior – my behavior – that's of import. In my mind's eye I can see myself reading the paper and rhythmically putting my hand in the chip bag, pulling out one chip at a time. And then my hand, with the chip in it, enters my mouth, over and over again – as if I were in a trance.

I don't know what made me stop before I finished the bag, maybe a vague awareness that my hand was going further and further down into it. When I did stop, however, I was shocked – not so much by the quantity, although I consumed more chips than I usually eat – but by the out-of-body quality of the experience – and by the logy sensation in my brain and the bloated feeling in my belly.

On the verge of my historical (and hysterical) reaction to overeating – yelling at myself for being an out of control, big fat pig, with no will power – I stopped myself. I ask my clients to stop their verbal self-abusive assaults and ask themselves what they have learned from their episodes of overeating. So what did I learn? I learned that I am still vulnerable to mindless eating under certain conditions. I learned that I cannot take for granted the skills and tools I teach others. In this case, I was tired, stressed, and challenged with so much to do in such a very short period of time. I promised myself that next year, I'll start planning and implementing sooner.

It seems to me that asking ourselves what we learned is a much better strategy than yelling at ourselves. Berating and belittling doesn't work. We shut down because the guilt is too overwhelming. We know this. So if there is a next time (and I hope for all of us that there isn't), maybe, just maybe, finding the meaning in our mindless overeating, figuring out in what ways we are vulnerable, and doing so with gentleness, will prevent us from – eating the whole thing.

Ilene Leshinsky

What Are Your Triggers?

I've been doing this for many, many years – following the philosophy of attuned eating, practicing what I preach in my *BodySense* groups. And yet every now and again, I find myself eating when I'm not hungry. And when that happens, I don't select healthy, nutritious foods, I go right for the mind-numbing, high sugar, high fat varieties.

I remember an incident a few years ago when I was preparing to have friends over for brunch. I'm not a good cook (although I make a great salad and set a lovely table), so I was ordering a quiche as the main part of the meal and I allowed myself to be talked into quite a few tasty-looking and expensive pastries. On the way home, my husband pointed out that I had spent the same amount of money on the dessert as I had on the main course. Shame immediately bubbled up from deep down inside me and I felt horrible. The wave of shame kept getting bigger and bigger and by the time we arrived at home, I couldn't wait for him to leave the house so I could stuff my face with at least one of those pastries. Two *BodySense* "no no's" – eating when I clearly was not hungry and sneak eating.

The moral of the story, as they say, is to know your triggers. Shame (an old, old issue for me) is clearly one of mine, as is feeling "entitled" to eat beyond satiety when I've been working hard. And if I had been really paying attention, I would have been aware that I was feeling uncomfortable while talking with the person taking my dessert order.

So what are your triggers? I hear boredom a lot. "I'm bored so therefore I eat", say many of my clients. What if I were to propose that many of us are uncomfortable just sitting and being still with ourselves and with our feelings – and we call it boredom. What if we know we should start a project that we don't really want to do but we eat instead and we call it boredom rather than procrastination. Or what if husband or child or co-worker says something that makes us sad or angry and we don't want to confront him or her, so we eat instead. What if we're out to eat for the first time in ages and the food is so good and the ambiance so relaxing that we eat until we're stuffed rather than ask for a take-out box – and enjoy another delicious meal the next day. What if we're lonely or sad?

I also hear "I'm addicted to food". The women who say that to me are not obsessing about salad or chicken broth or shredded wheat (without the sugar frosting). They're addressing how challenging it is for them to stay away from/ stop eating foods that are high in sugar, salt, and fat. And we now know, science tells us, that these foods change brain chemistry, trigger the pleasure centers in the brain, so no wonder we want them and more and more and more of them.

So along with our trigger emotions and situations, we also need to know our trigger foods. I've learned the hard way not to keep quantities of chocolate chip cookies in my house. Out of sight/ out of mind on one hand or the battle with urges and cravings on the other. I choose the former.

Whether selecting a life partner, a career, or making the decision to eat or not to eat, we all need a certain level of self-awareness. And when we practice self-awareness, we discover our triggers. So, what are yours?

Ilene Leshinsky

Yes, You Can Stop Eating!

So many women I know say something like this: I don't know when to stop eating. I need a zipper on my mouth and someone to pull it shut because I don't know how to stop. I'm out of control around food. I'm an addict and food is my drug of choice. These thoughts and feelings make us feel bad about ourselves. We're bright, accomplished women. We're good wives, mothers, employees, business owners, and we feel out of control around food.

What if we changed our belief system? What if we hold the belief that we can become the experts about our own bodies, that we can partner with our bodies and learn to eat when we're hungry and stop when we're comfortable?

I remember standing in front of a group of 90 women who were looking to me as their weight loss guru and feeling like a fraud. Why? Because in my mind, I had just "binged" on my fourth graham cracker. Not my fourth box, but my fourth cracker! It was at that moment that I realized that I needed to decide for myself what to eat, when to eat, and how much to eat. In other words, I could do this. I could develop a harmonious relationship with food and with my body. And those signals would come from within me. From this epiphany, BodySense was born and that was 15 years ago.

Here are the simple (but not necessarily easy) principles:

Eat whatever you want, keeping good nutrition in mind (I'll address this next month).

But eat only when you're hungry (explored in the April edition of Jill).

And stop when you're comfortable/ full. Not when someone else tells you to stop or the serving size on the package says you've had enough but when your internal satiety feeling says: time to stop. I've had enough. (I know, you don't believe you have one, but you do.)

Reflections of a Fat Girl

For some of us, though, enough is not enough. We have issues. We want food to fill our emotional abyss – and it can't – but we keep trying. We need to remember that food is just fuel for the body and not a salve for our emotional wounds. For others of us, we've conditioned ourselves to believe that other people are the experts about our bodies. "They" know what's best for us. And some of us have grown to believe that we can't trust ourselves, that our bodies will betray us. On all counts, how sad!

Take this leap of faith with me. You can learn to eat when you're hungry. And you can learn to stop when you're comfortable/ full. Here's a strategy that I've been using for the last fifteen years, ever since the graham cracker crisis.

I want you to picture an internal fuel gauge that is situated in your stomach and runs up to your breastbone. The numbers on the gauge read from zero to ten with zero being "ravenous" (I'm so hungry I can't think and I want to eat the whole supermarket) and ten being "stuffed" (so stuffed, I've made myself sick"). In the middle of the gauge is five which is "comfortable" (I could eat more, but I've had enough for now). So… if we eat mindfully, eating slowly, we can notice how our stomachs start to fill up as we move from a two – to a three – to a four – and to a five on the fuel gauge. At five we may be ready to stop eating, although some people feel better stopping at a six or a seven, which is in the "full" range. Notice we are not starting at a zero or a one, in the ravenous danger zone and we are not stopping at an eight or a nine or a ten, in the stuffed danger zone.

So try this fuel gauge strategy to determine when you are hungry and when you are comfortable/ full. As you use it, you will become an expert about your own body and your own hunger. Let me know if it works for you.

And finally, promise yourself, take a solemn vow, to feed yourself the very next time you get hungry!

Ilene Leshinsky

What Are We Really Hungry for?

On a Sunday afternoon in mid-July, I stood in front of a case of ice cream treats at a gas station convenience store in Millbury, Massachusetts. My husband and I were on our way home from a whirlwind visit with my family (one sister and her husband, one uncle, one niece and her partner, two great-nephews, and two great-nieces, one of them an adorable two month old and the real reason for the visit. I love my family and it was a great trip, but packed with activity, some sensitive negotiations, and no nap time for Ilene.

Back to Ilene at the frozen ice cream case. I confess. I was not hungry and ice cream certainly isn't a fuel food anyway. But I was feeling that I wanted something – something sweet. My "child-within", who remembers on a cellular level that sweets always distracted her from any form of discomfort, wanted an ice cream bar.

In her article "How to Tame the Wanting Mind" in the magazine "Shambhala Sun" (July 2011), author Sasha T. Loring explores three components to overcoming the cravings that lead to excessive consumption of food and other things as well. Firstly, she says, we need to "examine the wanting mind" by noticing when wanting goes beyond basic ordinary needs. This wanting can lead us to a sense, a feeling, of being fundamentally unfulfilled. "… Recognizing the 'I want' state of mind, letting it arise, looking at it, and letting it go [through the practice of meditation or other mindfulness practices] can bring a more settled and satisfying sense of equanimity into your life instead of being constantly subject to a never-ending series of desires." says Loring. Whether it's an ice cream treat, clothing, shoes, or designer bags, are we often in search of something to fill the hole inside of us?

I sit with many women in my **BodySense** practice who painfully talk about their perceived, insatiable hunger. A hunger for food - and lots of it – is how they initially describe the deep, ever-present hole inside of them. When we look inside that hole, however, we often see that what they hunger for has little or nothing to do with food. More love, more time for me, real connection, financial security, peace of mind, freedom from fear are some of the things they begin to realize are at the core of their all-consuming hunger.

The second aspect of diminishing craving is "loosening fixation". According to Loring, fixations keep our minds narrowly focused on the object of desire (my ice cream treat). Fixations have a way of "kidnapping" our minds, our attention, which we can deliberately take back through breath-centered practices. (Why didn't I think to do my yoga breaths before selecting the Magnum bar, surrounded by caramel and thickly coated with chocolate?)

And thirdly, we can overcome our cravings by learning how to transform them into an offering. When eating a meal, I leave a small portion of food on my plate, as a way of reminding myself physically and psychologically that I have had enough and that I am filled and satisfied. Loring mentally offers up that portion at the end of the meal, saying to herself, "May all beings have enough to eat". I so love this practice, which connects us to our sisters and brothers around the world. And, Loring instructs, the next time we're shopping for something we really don't need and we notice a craving, we might simply open our hand and offer up a wish that all beings have the warmth and comfort of what we desire. Loring says that this gesture can actually shift our brain activity from a "me" focus to a more openhearted and generous state of mind.

So the next time I have a wonderful, albeit stressful experience, and find myself in front of an ice cream case in Wherever, USA, or looking online for a designer bag that I do not need, I'll remember Sasha Loring's three steps to taming the wanting mind. I hope!

Ilene Leshinsky

If You're an Emotional Eater, Wait Ten Minutes!

I was in a car accident recently. It wasn't a big one and thank God no one was hurt. However, accidents are jolting and can make us feel very vulnerable. After the initial shock, I wanted to eat. For me and for many of us, food calms and soothes. It transports us from our fears, our anxieties, our angers, our discontent, to a place where nothing bad can touch us – at least for a few moments – or so we believe. (I forgot to tell you, I didn't eat.)

The origin of my emotional eating goes back many decades. I was a baby when Dr. Spock was telling mothers to feed their babies on a regular schedule and that healthy babies were round and plump. (No science back then about how fat cells are formed in infancy and can plague us for life!) So family lore goes that I was a finicky eater. My glamorous mother would try all kinds of tactics to make me laugh (including putting a mop on her head) so she could shove a spoonful of food into my open mouth. I learned very early that it pleased my mother if I ate. So I did. As I got older, and fell off my bike, got teased at school (for my weight), or had a fight with my sister, I was offered a cookie to make me feel better. So I made some important, albeit dangerous associations very early. Eating makes the people you love happy. And food heals hurts, both physical and emotional. (Can you relate?)

For many of us, we can make a connection between our eating behaviors now and what we learned in childhood. Pick up your own historical thread and follow it back in time. What beliefs about food did you learn? Some of my clients tell me that when they were little, food, like love, was rationed. The refrigerator and the cabinets were locked. They felt deprived and bereft. Others remember being the only ones at the dinner table with a "low cal" meal. They too felt deprived and many became sneak eaters. Yet others report turning to food for comfort. Their lives were filled with the chaos and crisis of some kind of abuse or addiction. So many of us learned that for a few moments in time, food could lift us from our circumstances to a place of comfort and love. Geneen Roth eloquently explores this connection in her book <u>When Food Is Love.</u>

Okay. So here we are with that very powerful association. What do we do now? We blame our mothers and we keep on eating. (Just kidding!) No, we learn to "remother" ourselves. We go back to basics and teach ourselves (as if we were little children again) that food is fuel for the body. We eat only when we are hungry, which is the body's way of signaling that it needs refueling. And…we find other ways to calm and soothe ourselves – without automatically turning to food.

So here's your homework. Make a list of ten things that calm and soothe you, other than food. Deep breathing should be #1 on the list. (There is no better anti-anxiety medication in the world than oxygen getting into the diaphragm.) Make the list realistic, things you can do within your means and lifestyle. Hugging my dog and my husband work great for me, as does going for a run. Your list should include things you can do right now (breathe, call a friend, have a good cry), and later (take a bubble bath, watch your favorite DVD, plan a vacation).

The next time you're upset and get the urge (you know, the urge to eat when you're not hungry) pull out your list. Start at the top and work down. Generally (and research supports this), if we can distract ourselves for ten minutes, the urge will pass. And we'll be so proud of ourselves. We calmed and soothed ourselves - without turning to food. Try it!

Ilene Leshinsky

Make Eating a Mindful Experience

A while ago, one of my clients gave birth and decided to breastfeed her infant so she often brought her baby to therapy. Sometimes in the middle of session, it was time to eat. I'd watch the baby start to cry, curl her fists, scrunch up her face, and make her little body rigid. She was hungry and she knew it. As her mother attended to that need, I'd watch the baby melt with pleasure into her mother, face and body relaxed, eyes closed as her needs were met, both physically and emotionally. Witnessing this, I could not doubt the powerful connection between food and emotions. Right from the beginning, food nourishes our bodies and nurtures our emotional selves.

But we're not babies anymore and life has gotten a little more complicated. Nutritious food is not going to magically appear when we're hungry. I hear so many women say that they don't have time to eat. Other women say that they don't receive or recognize hunger signals. They use the clock to signal that it's time to feed themselves. Others share that they don't realize that they've reached for food until they've swallowed the last bite of Danish that was sitting on the office or kitchen counter. This is how disconnected we are from our bodies! (As an aside, please… if you're going to eat that Danish, do it slowly, mindfully, and joyously relish every single bite.)

Some women tell me that they don't have food "issues", that they just love food and love to eat. So after a long day at work and then numerous family responsibilities at home, when they find themselves snacking in the kitchen at midnight, too exhausted to care what they're eating, they say they simply love food. Right? Well, I don't think so. I believe that the above scenario happens as a way of saying: This is my time. This is my reward for getting through another day packed with doing things for everyone else but me! Is this a conscious thought? Probably not. The point is that for so many of us, our eating behaviors are mindless. For whatever reasons, we find our hand in the proverbial cookie jar and we don't know how it got there. What I am suggesting, however, is that something indeed happened five minutes or five hours before we found the cookie (or Danish) in our mouths.

Picture this scenario. You're roaming the kitchen (home or office) looking for something to eat. Nothing seems appealing – or that piece of Danish starts calling your name. Either way, you can go down one of two paths.

- Path One: You eat the Danish (my guess is quickly with minimal chewing involved). You realize what you've done and then beat yourself up for the rest of the day, reinforcing that you are a piglet and out of control around food.

- Path Two: You ask yourself if you're hungry, true body hunger. If the answer is yes… more choices. Will the Danish fuel your body, giving you the energy you need to successfully complete your day? Is there something else that will? (You know the answer. This is not a trick question.) If the answer is no, then you can ask yourself why you want to eat when you know you're not hungry. Please don't land on "I don't know." You may not want the answer, but you know. You might have to spend a few moments thinking and feeling. However, on the other side of those moments you might realize that a project deadline is stressing you out or you don't know how to handle your teenager who has been withdrawing from the family or you feel upset by an argument you had with your partner or you're worried about your family's financial future.

Knowing the answer isn't necessarily going to change your life (although you just might point yourself in the right direction). But…eating when you're not hungry won't change your life either. And…it will only make you feel bad (or worse) about yourself. So please, don't go there!

Ilene Leshinsky

Feeding the Holiday Heart

It's holiday time again, when Christmas, Chanukah, Kwanzaa, and Festivus (remember the Seinfeld episode?) bring family and friends together. Some say for a season of love and togetherness, and sadly, others say for a few weeks of overspending and overeating. For some it is a time when the world makes itself beautiful and the people in it are kinder and more loving. For others it's a season that underscores their unhappiness, their loneliness, and their disconnections from family and friends.

Raise your hand if you grew up in a Hallmark Card family. You know, the kind that isn't affected by physical or mental health problems. The kind where all the children get good grades and are not involved with drugs and alcohol. Where there are no financial issues. Where mom and dad are having a respectful and warm relationship with each other. Where the house is always clean, dusted and vacuumed – by mom of course, who also works full time, chauffeurs her kids to practice, and puts a home cooked meal on the table every night (which the family actually sits down and eats together).

Now raise your hand if you did not grow up in the above scenario. How does this time of year make you feel? I don't want to sound like a holiday spirit buster but as a teller of the truth, I think it is absolutely necessary to acknowledge that many of us did not grow up with, or do not have now, a Hallmark family.

It dawned on me the other day that maybe we get messages about what the holidays should be like, how families should operate, in the same ways we have come to believe that our bodies should look a certain way. From the media!

Now I'm not blaming television commercials, TV programs or magazine ads for our holiday depression or minimally our sense of disappointment at holiday time. But I am saying that it's easy to get caught up in the wishes, hopes, and fantasies that our lives should be like those Hallmark families. We absorb these images in the same way we absorb the ones that promise that we, too, can have the perfect body. And... we are left wanting, feeling deficient, and on the outside looking in. I used to eat my way through the month of December. The oh so numbing effects of high fat, high sugar foods, that I hoped would disconnect me from my feelings and from the circumstances of my life. (Some of you know exactly what I am talking about.)

Holidays bring up our stuff – past and present. They certainly do! However, just like at any other moment in time, we have a choice – a choice to eat our way into oblivion or to find other ways to feed our holiday hearts – the ones that remember the past and long for something different (or for some of us, the same) in the present. I know this is easier said than done, really, I know, but can we try something different this year.

Feed your physical self with food, not your emotional one.

Volunteer at a soup kitchen, a school, or an animal shelter.

Create a new tradition – dinner with your family by choice (which may be different than your family by blood).

Visit patients in the hospital or in a nursing home.

Start that book you've been dying to read.

Phone or e-mail that friend you've been meaning to reconnect with.

Write in your journal or on your gratitude list.

Buy or make yourself a present.

Doing something different is not going to change history, but it very well may change your relationship with it. And you may find that come January 2, 2011, you haven't gained those usual seven to ten pounds holiday pounds.

Ilene Leshinsky

Emotional Eating: The Good, the Bad, and the Tasty

I have vivid memories of being a child of around nine years old and ducking into the corner variety store for my "appetizer" of candy bars – before lunch. My mother later told me that she would watch me walk down the street to our house, eating the candy bars in what she described as a sneaky way. She never said anything at the time and my desire, need, habit of eating emotionally and secretly would last for many years. I was unhappy, my family was unhappy and I was treating my symptoms of unhappiness with high sugar, high fat foods – a pattern that would stay with me into adulthood.

You've heard me say repeatedly that we were born knowing how to eat. Just watch a baby signal its hunger and then its satiety and you will know without question that this is true.

There is another aspect of eating that also is integrally linked with hunger and eating and that is our desire for comfort. From birth, babies take comfort when they are held while being fed. You can see an infant melt into the arms of its mother or father, its eyes closing, often dropping off to sleep. Yes, comfort is also programmed into our experience of food.

So if we're innately programmed for both hunger and comfort, what's the big deal if we eat emotionally? Recently one of my clients sent me an article from Real Simple.com entitled, "The Facts about Emotional Eating" that explores this issue and suggests that emotional eating is not all that bad – sometimes.

Numerous studies indicate that foods rich in carbohydrates, sugars, and fats not only taste delicious but increase mood and decrease anxiety, at least temporarily. Many of us have experienced how certain foods can transport our bodies and brains to a "better" place. However, according to the article, a 2012 study from the University of Montreal Hospital Research Centre showed that after twelve weeks, mice that were fed on a higher fat diet showed more signs of depression and anxiety than those fed lower amounts.

You don't have to be a lab rat to agree with the outcome of this study. Many of us know firsthand the mind-altering effects of high fat, high sugar foods, and the negative physical and emotional consequences of eating those foods.

The late, great Nora Ephron is quoted in the article. She says, "I have made a lot of mistakes falling in love, and regretted most of them, but never the potatoes that went with them". If only all of us could be so philosophical and so self-accepting– and not so judgmental!

Here are some questions that might help us determine if we're overdoing emotional eating:

~ Do you frequently eat when you feel emotional but not particularly hungry?

~ Instead of confronting a problem, do you hit the refrigerator?

~ Do you punish yourself after having a treat?

~ Do you regularly overeat those carby, fatty foods?

These are simple check-ins and worth taking a few minutes to assess. It's so important, however, to look at our eating behaviors with curiosity, with gentleness – without judgment. No learning can ever occur when we're berating and belittling ourselves!

My unhappy, nine year old self would have answered yes to all of the above. And she certainly experienced the negative physical and psychological consequence of emotional eating as a primary coping mechanism. I now look at her with so much compassion. She was a child with so few options. My adult self, however, with lots of patience and practice, would answer those questions with the word "seldom". But when I do eat when I'm not hungry, sometimes, like Nora Ephron, I go right for the mashed potatoes – or the chocolate.

Ilene Leshinsky

Food, Glorious Food!

I love food! And I love to eat! I know that there are people in the world – and in my family – who do not really care about food. They tell me they eat to live, to fuel their bodies, to have energy to work and play. I get that. It's Principle #1 of BodySense. What I don't get is anyone not relishing the tastes and textures, the aromas, the physical presentation, the beauty of a plate of delectable food.

I was told that as an infant and toddler that I was not a good eater. I can't even imagine this but family lore says it is true. My grandmother on my father's side, my Bubbie, would complain to my mother that I was too thin. My thighs and arms didn't have enough meat on them! So my mom, to please my grandmother, would put a mop on her head. I would laugh and mom would shove a spoonful of something into my mouth. That nightly ritual taught me some important but faulty messages: my eating makes my mother happy and less anxious; eating is not correlated with hunger; food tastes great. Years later, it was hard to fathom the very opposite messages of: Ilene, you're eating too much; you don't need a second helping; you're getting too fat. Reconciling my love of food and retraining myself to eat from hunger have been my life's work – personally and professionally.

This is the season of abundance – of food (and so much of it high in fat and sugar), of partying, shopping, and spending. It's challenging at best to let our bodies lead, to pay attention to true body hunger signals in this season of excess, in which each of us is predicted to gain seven to ten pounds between Thanksgiving and the New Year's Day.

Giada de Laurentis, a famous chef on the Food Network and a contributor to the Today Show, spends all day, every day, with food – and she's tiny. In a recent interview in Spry Magazine (distributed by the Press-Republican) she says that in Italy the portion sizes are small, much smaller than in the US so people don't eat as much. And she also says that when confronted with a large selection of food, she eats just a little of what she likes. Good advice for this holiday season, don't you think?

In the title song, "Food, Glorious Food" from the musical Oliver, the young boys in the orphanage fantasize about eating food – real food – glorious food – not the small amounts of tasteless gruel they receive. They're always hungry, always wanting more.

What are we wanting more of? For most of us – and aren't we blessed – food is in abundance and we are not starving. Yet we live and participate in a culture of overabundance and overindlgence. When we overeat at this time of year – or at any time – what are we really wanting? I ask this of my BodySense clients: When I eat when I'm not hungry – and I eat so much that I've made myself sick – what do I really want?

Their answers were my answers: I eat to stuff my feelings – my anger, my sadness, my fear, my shame; I eat because I feel hopeless and helpless; I eat because I feel so all alone; I eat because there's never enough time for me; I eat because I'm grieving the loss of a loved one; I eat because I was betrayed. The answers and the list could go on and on.

What I had to teach myself and what I hope I pass on to my clients is that actually, food doesn't fix anything – not any of our emotional wounds that need healing, that is. Yes, for a few seconds it transports us to a place free from worry and sadness, but then we're left with those same problems and hurts – and added weight, more health issues, and feeling really, really bad about ourselves.

So this holiday season – and into the New Year – can we make a vow to put food in its proper place? Food is fuel for the body and brain! Delicious fuel, glorious fuel, but fuel nonetheless. Without it our ancestors would not have survived and we wouldn't be here to grapple with our very complicated relationship with food. And not to be a holiday party pooper, but just for the record, cake, gingerbread cookies, pies, ice cream, doughnuts, éclairs, and chips and dip – are not fuel!

Ilene Leshinsky

I'm Hungry!

I have a friend who tells me that she is always hungry. That even after a filling meal, she is hungry for more. Over the years I have respectfully disagreed with her, that after consuming a filling meal, she couldn't possibly want more to eat. However, her insistence that she's still hungry has encouraged me to look at the many definitions of hunger and what we mean when we say "I'm hungry."

When I was a kid, I would have agreed with my friend. I felt I was always hungry. I believed I was always hungry. However, as an adult, and through the eyes and training of a therapist, I see myself and the issue differently. Yes, I was starving. Yes, I needed to be filled. But with food? Always with food? Everything I know from my research and from my own experience says that my body – most bodies – (well maybe not my friend's body) gets hungry and when I feed it, does not signal hunger again for three to five hours.

I hear many of my clients say that they have no willpower, no self-discipline. They feel they don't have what it takes to just stop eating. I used to say the same things, use the same language to describe my out-of-control eating. However, I believe they are wrong. I was wrong.

Remember the Calgon Bath Oil commercial? The one that depicted a woman in a bathtub surrounded by bubbles? Remember her lying back in the tub dreamily saying, "Calgon, take me away."? What did she want to be taken away from? The stress of her life? Worry about her kids? Financial problems? A challenging relationship with her spouse? Aging without fulfilling the dreams she had earlier in life?

So many of us have used food, use food now to "take us away", to transport us to a different place, to tamp down the desire, the craving for a different life, one that will fill us up, satisfy us, give us pleasure. And if it's not food we're using to fill the hole in our bellies – or our hearts – it's alcohol or drugs or sex or shopping or even exercise. We have hungers, cravings, desires, and longings.

What do we do with them? What do we do when we feel frustrated and angry and disappointed that our lives haven't turned out the way we planned?

Well that question is the subject of another session – oops, article! But for now, I'm suggesting that we take a more direct approach, a straighter path, although maybe a more challenging one.

What actually do we hunger for? What are our desires, our longings? A loving relationship? A fulfilling career? A simpler lifestyle? More time to travel, to read a book, to paint or sew or write? More down time? Less stress? If we hunger for any of the above or for anything else not on the list, it seems to me that the pursuit of any one of them might be more productive and rewarding than any distraction we might be using to fill ourselves up.

I think we all have hungers, longings, cravings. Sometimes they are so strong, we can almost taste them! When I was a child, although I would not have been able to articulate this then, I hungered for a peaceful and loving home environment. When I was a young adult, I longed for a happy and fulfilling relationship. Now, as an older adult (in extended middle age), blessed with both, I crave warmer winters – and like Sandra Bullock's Gracie Lou Freebush in "Miss Congeniality" – I really do want world peace.

And sometimes if the truth be told, my taste buds come alive with thoughts of peanut butter pandemonium ice cream and chocolate chip cookies – and I eat them!

Ilene Leshinsky

Chapter 3:
You Can't Fool Body Wisdom… So, Why Not Follow Yours?

When I was in full-time private practice, I remember the day that one of my clients brought her newborn baby girl into our session. She was breastfeeding and very attentive to her daughter's cries for food. In the midst of the session that little baby cried and fussed. Both mother and baby knew what she wanted.

I watched as mom gave her breast to her daughter and how that little one melted into her mother's arms, and nursed and nursed, until she had had enough. And then, she fell asleep. My client told me that her daughter would sometimes push her breast away or turn her head when she was done eating. Watching that client and her daughter reinforced my understanding of intuitive eating, the way of eating that says: **We are born knowing how to eat.**

This chapter is about innate body wisdom, how eating is ingrained in each of us and is one of the wisdoms that our bodies hold.

Other wisdoms of the body are, believe it or not, how much we should weigh, how much sleep we need, how our bodies are made to move, as well as signals of danger and how negative self-talk harms the brain.

There's so much wisdom in this chapter!

Ilene Leshinsky

Find Your Own Way

As I write this article in late December, the annual influx of television commercials and magazine ads for weight loss programs has begun. Supplements, frozen foods, points, meal cards, meal replacements, on-line calculators, exercise machines, videos, balls and bands. Some promote themselves using celebrities (You, too, can look like Mariah Carey, Jennifer Hudson, and Janet Jackson). Some just use us ordinary folk. All of them, however, send the same message - that our lives will be transformed by weight loss. T'is the season of the weight loss hype – after the season of holiday weight gain.

All of these commercials send a subtle and not so subtle message that we women can't do it on our own, can't find our own way to health and well-being. (Notice I said health and well- being – not body beautiful. And all of them send the message that changing our bodies will change our lives, when what really changes our lives is making ourselves a priority and taking good care of ourselves, every day, for the rest of our lives.

Did you know that we were born knowing how to eat? Just watch an infant and you will never doubt the innate wisdom of the body again. That baby signals mom when she is hungry and pushes away the bottle or breast when she has had enough. If you're a mom with more than one child, you've probably noticed that your children have different eating patterns and schedules. And as they got older, they had different food preferences, as well. And so it is with us.

What makes me mad about the commercials, the products, and the programs is that they imply that we can't figure this weight management thing on our own. And they send the message that we have the appetites of out of control, wild beasts. What makes me the maddest is that we have come to believe, we've been brainwashed, that we have to turn our personal power over to someone else who knows our bodies and brains better than we do. If that were the case, why do we start diets and exercise programs and then stop them? Why do 95% of people who go on diets gain their weight back within two to five years? Because we're wild beasts? Because we lack any degree of will power or self-control? Absolutely not! The majority of us can't stay on a diet because it's not our way, the way that works in harmony with our body's natural rhythms and hunger cycles. Diets are based on calorie restriction and deprivation that may work for a while, but then our bodies rebel. Extreme exercise works for a while and then our bodies cannot sustain that energy expenditure – and we quit.

Am I giving us permission to eat nonstop without attention to nutrition? Am I giving us permission to ignore the knowledge and the wisdom that science now offers us. A resounding no! But if we're really honest with ourselves and mindful of our thoughts, feelings, and behaviors, we know – we absolutely know - that certain foods make us feel energized and other ones make us feel ready for a nap. We know that our brains and bodies work better with appropriate amounts of restorative sleep and with exercise that we can sustain regularly. We also know when we're eating to calm and soothe ourselves from the emotional stress of our busy and often chaotic lives rather than to fuel our bodies with nutritious foods. Take a guess? How many calories a day would we eliminate from our daily consumption if we ate only when we were truly hungry and we stopped when we were comfortable?

In our heart of hearts we know that following the path to body beautiful makes us feel sad, deficient, and less than. And following the one toward health and well-being makes us feel alive. So I encourage each of you to find your own way. Certainly, allow the knowledge and wisdom of others to guide you, to instruct, to shine light down the path to health, both physical and mental. And please choose a way of eating and exercising that you can do for life. If you choose the right ones – the foods for you, the exercise regimen for you, you'll know it. Your brain and body will sing in harmony. If not – well you'll know that too.

Ilene Leshinsky

Exploring the Innate Wisdom of the Body

Sometimes I feel like a salmon, swimming upstream to fulfill its biological imperative, getting bloodied and battered in the process. Although my spawning days are long gone, I do feel pushed, compelled, called, however, to send the message to any woman (or man) willing to listen: Our bodies, your body and mine, have innate wisdom. Among many things, they will tell us when to eat, what to eat, and when to stop.

In the midst of the profusion of diet and weight loss programs, this message of the quiet wisdom of the body often gets lost. Did you see the non stop commercials in January? Back to back ads promising weight loss and body perfection through teas, pills, supplements, and a myriad of exercise programs.

Don't get me wrong, I'm a believer in taking control of our individual health. We all know the negative consequences of obesity. Chronic illnesses, a shortened life span are just two. However, it's important to remember that there are many women who are considered "plus size" by the fashion industry, women whose numbers (blood pressure, glucose, hdl, ldl, triglycerides) are within normal range and who are considered healthy.

As a society, though, how did we get so large, so unhealthy? How did we disconnect from the innate wisdom of the body? There are many theories out there, but I will offer you a few.

~ Bodies were made to move. Otherwise we wouldn't have arms and legs. But we don't move regularly. We sit in front of the TV at night and snack. Our kids are on the computer instead of the playground. And our lives are so stressed and overextended that we don't have the physical or emotional energy to exercise.

~ We let others tell us how much food is enough for us. On one hand, diet programs tell us to restrict our calories for weight loss success (a set up for weight gain, by the way). On the other hand, restaurants serve us double and triple the portions we need to feel comfortable/ full. And we eat what they tell us to eat or put in front of us!

~ Bodies and brains need nutritious foods (complex carbs, proteins, good fats, fruits and vegetables) to function at optimal levels. They respond like race car engines when given proper fuel and sputter along when we eat doughnuts for breakfast. But we are often lured by the drug-like effects and the yummy tastes of high fat, high sugar, high salt foods.

Why do we override our innate wisdom and want to fast track our way to body beautiful or to a life of ease? Here's my take on the answer. We are a quick fix society. It's so hard to sit with our anxiety, our discomfort. We want to fit in. We want relief. So we go on a diet, take a pill, eat a cookie, have a drink, get a new spouse, buy a new car, and expect that all of our physical and emotional issues will go away. And here's the rub… they often do! But only for a few minutes! The truth is that the quick fixes just don't work for the long haul. And we know this. Deep down inside, in our wisdom place, we know this.

But we live in a society that tries to sell us magic. Every day, on TV, in magazines, we see thin, beautiful, smiling women, with flawless faces and bodies, selling us something that promises to make our lives better, easier, and happier. (Oh, by the way, you too could be in one of those ads if you had a make-up artist, hair stylist, and clothing designer. If you were airbrushed, photo-shopped, and elongated!)

I've said this before and I will until my last breath, we are the magic. The magic is the innate wisdom of our bodies, yours and mine. I challenge you to pay attention, learn the language, and respond accordingly.

Ilene Leshinsky

Body Healthy/ Body Beautiful

We've all gone through it – the dreaded plateau. We've been dieting and exercising for weeks, maybe months, and been exhilarated by our initial weight loss and energy surge. And then - nothing. No movement on the scale and we start to feel like failures. We must be doing something wrong. We should continue to be losing weight, we think, if our "calories in" (what we eat) continue to be less than our "calories out" (what we expend through exercise and just living our lives).

Conventional wisdom and those who promote it tell us to eat a little less, or eat different foods, or exercise a little more, or find different ways to exercise. So we do a combination of the above, feel gratified that the scale starts to move in the right direction – and then it happens again. Plateau #2 or #22. At some point most of us, already feeling like failures, just quit.

There's another explanation for our inability to shed unwanted pounds and that's the concept of Set Point. Set Point theory tells us that our bodies have a weight range (usually 5 – 10 pounds) in which they feel comfortable, based on our genetics and lifestyle factors such as the amount we regularly exercise, how physically demanding our jobs are, and the nutritional quality of the foods we eat. When we try to manipulate our caloric intake and expenditure below our comfortable range, our bodies will rebel. They will perceive the decrease of calories as famine, the same way our cave dweller ancestors perceived the times when food was in short supply. They will rebel by slowing down and burning fewer calories. No wonder we stop losing weight. Oh no, we say. But I want to be thinner and sexier! So our minds tell us to try a new diet and our bodies continue to keep us in our set point range or at our natural weight.

I had this "ah ha" moment the other day, that at sixty-four years old, I weigh five pounds less than I did when I graduated from high school at seventeen. My set point? Maybe. At seventeen, however, I thought I was fat and unlovable. Years of cultural and family messages created the recipe for those beliefs, leading to decades of "yo-yo" dieting, from highly restrictive eating to compulsive overeating behaviors. At sixty-four, however, I now see myself as a healthy and yes, pretty woman, with curves, a great smile, and so much love and wisdom to offer my family, my friends, my clients, and my community. I feel so bad for what I put myself through at those other stages of my life. The obese little girl, the sneak-eating adolescent, the young adult who firmly believed that the ticket to love was only bought by a thin and toned body.

In all of those life-stage iterations of me, I was wrong! The only way to true, long-lasting happiness is through self-love, self-care, and body acceptance. Is it an on-going challenge for those of us who naturally do not fit into the socio-cultural ideal of beauty? Absolutely yes! However, the negative physical and emotional health consequences of not doing so are far too great. We can continue the diet/ weight gain cycle that leads to increased stress, negative self-worth, and inflammation in our blood vessels or we can examine our current health habits. Are we giving ourselves appropriate amounts of restorative sleep, nutritious food choices that fuel our bodies, regular amounts of aerobic and weight bearing exercise? And then, can we accept, can we embrace that where our bodies land, with those health habits in place routinely, is where our bodies are meant to be? At our set point? At our natural weight?

With the skyrocketing rise in life-threatening eating disorders in females and males, are we ready, as a society, for a paradigm shift? I certainly hope so!

Ilene Leshinsky

On Your Mark… Get Set… Go to Your Natural Weight!

The last time that I participated in an organized weight loss program was about thirty years ago, but I remember the experience as if it was yesterday. "What number do you want as your goal weight?" asked the receptionist at my first visit. I chose a number that I had weighed after my divorce when I was too miserable to eat and very skinny, by the way.

Has this ever happened to you? You go on a diet or a program and expect to lose x amount of pounds and weigh ____ (fill in the blank). You choose a number that you weighed when you were in the fifth grade or when you were twenty years old, with little consideration of how realistic that number is today. And then at some point on your weight loss journey you stop losing weight and you think the problem is you and your lack of willpower. Yes?

Set Point theory says that our inability to lose that last ten, twenty or more pounds may not be about our lack of self-control but about our body's way of finding its natural weight. Set Point theory is the weight your body comfortably settles at when you're eating in response to hunger, stopping when full, and engaging in some degree of regular, physical activity. So two women could be the same height, eat about the same amount of food and weigh different amounts.

Linda Bacon, a nutrition and weight regulation physiologist, in her book *Health at Every Size: The Surprising Truth about Your Weight*, says that Set Point is a force that pulls us back to a comfortable range for our bodies when we veer away. Dieting does exactly the opposite. It intentionally pulls us away from our body's comfortable range. And… through dieting, when we override our signals of hunger and fullness again and again and again, this natural system becomes broken. (Does this explain why every time I stopped dieting I landed at just about the same size and weight I'm at now?)

The goal, therefore, is to find **your** healthy weight! According to Judith Matz, LCSW, in her article "Recipe for Life" in the

January/February edition of **Psychotherapy Networker**, and contrary to what we hear from much of the medical community, "people who diet are eight times as likely to develop eating disorders, score higher on measurements of stress and depression compared to nondieters and experience greater health risks such as cardiovascular disease and Type 2 diabetes as a result of weight cycling." So dieting can be damaging to our physical and mental health? According to some of the latest research, yes!

Am I giving us permission to throw away our knowledge of healthy eating and to consume a diet high in sugars, fats, and salts? Absolutely not! What I am saying is that we were born knowing how to eat. Babies cry when they are hungry and turn away from the breast or bottle when they've had enough. Can we get back to that early, attuned awareness of how to feed ourselves?

Attuned or intuitive eating doesn't mean eating whatever you want, whenever you want, and as much as you want. It guides you and me to eat what the body is hungry for, when it's hungry, choosing from a wide variety of nutritious foods. Attuned eating allows us to reestablish a natural, anxiety-free relationship with food. And when we do and we sprinkle in some regular exercise, we'll find ourselves at our set point, at our natural weight. Sounds good to me!

Ilene Leshinsky

To Eat or Not to Eat: That Is the Question

How do we know if we're hungry?

Have you ever had the experience of eating foods that you love when you are genuinely, physically hungry? When your body has signaled you that it is hungry? If you have, then you know that eating from hunger, from true physical hunger, is one of the most joyous experiences in the world. Food tastes wonderful and our bodies and brains are energized! But how do we know if we are truly hungry? Women ask me this question all the time.

Our bodies, in their innate wisdom, send us hunger signals. Just like the little tank on the gas gauge that lights up before we run out of gas and are left stranded on the side of the road, our bodies send us hunger signals so that we don't run out of gas, so that we don't run out of the ability to think clearly and move energetically.

Some of us don't have a clue about hunger because we've spent so long trying to control it or push it away. We've used coffee, cigarettes or diet soda to keep a lid on our hunger. On the other end of the continuum, some of us have never given our bodies enough time to get hungry. We've eaten compulsively for a variety of reasons, including fear of experiencing true body hunger.

What are your hunger signals? Everyone experiences hunger differently, but there are some commonalities. Common signals are: a feeling of emptiness in the stomach; stomach noises, gurgling or growling; lightheadedness; headaches; shakiness in one's hands, arms, and legs; feelings of nausea, difficulty thinking, irritability.

But how often do we women ignore our hunger signals? Some of us have come to believe that hunger awakens the insatiable beast inside of us. The second we put food in our mouths that beast will keep us eating nonstop and will not/ cannot be satisfied. So…we don't eat. We put off eating or we starve ourselves. I used to be one of those women who would not eat breakfast (and sometimes lunch) thinking that I would be cutting my calorie intake for the day significantly if I ate fewer meals. In truth, I was consuming more calories later in the day because I was starving and… I was obsessed with thoughts and images of food throughout the day. (Can you relate?)

So if we eat when we're hungry, we'll awaken the insatiable beast. Right? Wrong, so very wrong! We can teach our bodies to trust us when we respond to the hunger signals that they send. We do that by feeding them.

But I eat all the time, you say. I eat when I'm hungry, when I'm sad, lonely, depressed, tired. I eat when I'm happy, bored, and anxious. You're not alone and you're addressing the difference between body hunger and mind hunger. True body hunger sends the aforementioned signals and those signals arise from your body. Body hunger comes in regular intervals, three to five hours after the last eating experience. Mind hunger, on the other hand, does not have physical symptoms and does not come in regular intervals. Body hunger is a signal that the body is low on fuel. Mind hunger signals that the emotional self is in need of something. What does the emotional self need…love, comfort, companionship, compassion, support? We're not going to know unless we're willing to ask.

So, to eat or not to eat is no longer a challenging question. Let's honor our bodies by feeding them when they are physically hungry. And let's honor our psyches by bravely asking them what they need and responding appropriately.

Ilene Leshinsky

Are You on a Diet – Again?

Did I ever tell you about the moment that *BodySense* was born? I was leading a meeting of ninety women in Brookline, Massachusetts in the spring of 1992, all of those wonderful women wanting to lose weight with this national program and all of them looking to me for the keys to the weight loss kingdom because I was their leader. So I'm giving the lesson of the week, and I'm looking out onto a sea of lovely faces who are looking back at me because they think that I have the answers. But I'm thinking, "Ilene, you are such a hypocrite and a fraud! You're offering guidance that you cannot even follow yourself." I had just binged.

So what did this binge entail, you might be wondering? OMG... I had just eaten four graham crackers – not four boxes, not four cellophane-wrapped packages within the box, but four crackers! That's not a binge, Ilene, you may be thinking – and of course you would be right. But in my mind, at that moment, it was, because it was not the number of crackers that constituted the plan's "serving size". And in that moment, I was struck by my irrational thinking and a light bulb went off. Maybe, just maybe, I could learn to trust myself. Maybe my body held wisdom to communicate to me when to eat, what to eat, and how much to eat. It was then, with lots of reading and research, that I found the philosophy of intuitive eating. It was then that *BodySense* was born.

Did you know that only five people in a hundred achieve success on diets? We frequently hear the statistic that 95% of people who go on diets gain back their weight in one to five years. Now translate that into how many people are actually successful. Five! Five out of a hundred! And why? Because the ninety-five people are lazy sloths? Because they lack will power and or self-control? Or, because diets set up a conflictual relationship between ourselves and our bodies. It's not just because they are based on reduced calories and disallow our favorite foods. It's because diets disconnect us from our bodies – from the innate wisdom that they hold.

In the 1980's, female (and feminist) authors began writing about the negative – and temporary – effects of dieting. Suzie Orbach, Susan Kano, Carol Munter, Jane Hirschman, and Geneen Roth promised freedom from conflicts with weight, eating and body image issues and freedom to create a life filled with joy, passion, and creativity. And they were right! And they continue to be my heroes – my goddesses.

What I had to grapple with was my changing body. The process forced me to take many leaps of faith as I learned that giving myself permission to eat chocolate chip cookies did not mean that eating the whole bag was what my body wanted or needed. And the "experts" were right. High fat, high sugar foods are not good sources of energy - and they promote weight gain! And oh my God, I gained weight – and then I lost weight as I paid attention to my body's hunger and satiety signals.

What intuitive eating promises is that our bodies will find their "natural weight" or "set point". When we're eating when we are truly, physically hungry, eating a variety of healthy, nutritious foods, stopping when we have reached satiety (not stuffed), and we are moving/ exercising regularly, our bodies will reward us by achieving natural weight. Not ideal weight – what we might want to weigh to fit into today's cultural ideal of beauty – but a weight at which our bodies are comfortable and our minds are free to live life fully, without constant thoughts of food and without hunger pains because we're trying to shave a few more calories from our eating day. Natural weight takes into account our genetic makeup and our lifestyle. We may not be able to alter our genetics (I will never be tall) but we can certainly make healthier and more intelligent lifestyle choices regarding food selections and exercise modalities.

And my body found its natural weight. For twenty plus years, I've been just about the same size and weight. The obese little girl who sneaked candy bars on her way home to eat lunch, the overweight adolescent struggling to fit in with her family and peer group, the lost young woman trying and failing every diet known to womankind - all of these "me's" are now at peace. I discovered that because of my body's innate wisdom, I was born knowing how to eat. And so were you!

Ilene Leshinsky

Body Language

So… what do you think (about this or that or whatever)? How many times have we been asked that question in our lives? And using the amazing power of our brains, we analyze, we deliberate and we come up with an answer. Yes? And in our western culture in which we revere mind over matter, this is how we make decisions.

Call it intuition, call it a gut reaction, call it a felt sense or a body knowing, we receive important information from a place other than our minds. If we're relying solely on our minds to make decisions, we're missing out on another source of wisdom – the inner knowing that comes from our bodies.

When I was a junior in college, many moons ago, I was attacked one night while walking from the trolley stop to my apartment. It was 11:00 at night and the street was deserted except for me - and a man walking towards me. (I know, I know! I should never have been out alone, in Boston at that hour. But in my defense, I grew up in a neighborhood where we didn't lock our doors – even at night.) I remember, as if it were yesterday, alarm bells going off in my body. No thoughts, just body sensations that made every cell vibrate with "Danger! Danger!"

I am thankful that it was not a sexual assault, nor even a robbery as I had a large amount of cash in my purse, but the incident left me shaken for months – and even years to come. Few people in the 1960's were identifying post-traumatic stress symptoms – and I couldn't understand why I was unable to walk down the street by myself, even in broad daylight, why I couldn't be alone in my apartment, and why I couldn't comprehend a paragraph in one of my textbooks, even after reading it over and over again. It took a long time for me to feel somewhat safe again, in my home, and in my world. The gift from that experience is that I now pay very close attention to my body signals – and I no longer walk down dark and empty streets alone.

Recently, a client said to me, when talking about her first

husband, who was controlling and an alcoholic, "I should have run in the opposite direction", firstly when he asked her to go out on a date, and then secondly when he asked her to marry him. She had a negative, visceral response – but ignored it! Now, she, too, is so much better at listening to her body language.

From that same place in my brain – from hers and from yours – comes the inner knowing of when to eat, what to eat, and how much to eat. Since eating is a major part of survival and survival is the main function of the limbic brain, our hunger signals are sent to us automatically from that brain center. I hope we will all remember this when we know we're hungry, but choose to ignore the signals because of our desire to restrict calories. In the days of our cave dweller ancestors, Ben and Jerry were not making ice cream, and cheesecake, doughnuts, and chocolate chip cookies did not exist. Our ancestors did not have to choose from sweet treats or fuel foods. But we do! After years of experimentation, it is clear to me that my body negatively reacts to high fat, high sugar foods when I'm hungry, with stomach cramps, brain surges and then resulting lethargy. My body communicates the negative effects of empty calories and the positive effects of nutritious ones. My guess is that so does yours.

A Vermont woman wrote a letter to the editor in "Seven Days" newspaper about a few months ago. I'm quoting her because I think her message is so important. "Dietary fads and recommendations come and go, but what is most important in determining my health is listening to my body… First I placed too much power in the hands of those selling the yummy fatty/ sugar foods. Then I placed too much power into the hands of the experts. Finally, I placed the power in the wisdom of my own body."

Whether we're talking about warning signals regarding our safety or knowing when to eat and what to eat, our bodies are powerful communicators – if we choose to listen to them. We humans are exquisite processing machines. Mind, body, and spirit can work together to guide us through life. Let's make sure we tap into all of our wisdom sources.

Ilene Leshinsky

Listen to Your Body Talk

Do you believe in magic? "… In a young girl's heart, how the music can free her whenever it starts?" as the song by the Lovin' Spoonful goes. I do! I believe there is magic and mystery all around us. Some say coincidence. I say magic. That belief keeps me young and expecting great things for myself and for everyone else.

What I don't believe in is body magic – the external messages we continually receive that promise that we can transform our bodies into those of movie stars, supermodels, and professional athletes. While we're watching television or flipping through a magazine we are bombarded with images and products, promising flat abs, thin thighs, tens of pounds of weight loss, if only we'll pay our money and then pop a pill or religiously follow a particular program. We want to believe so we buy into the hype.

Here's the real magic! Our bodies hold the wisdom to transform us from sickness to health, from obesity to natural weight, from obsession to freedom. Can you take this leap of faith with me? Our bodies are our friends, our allies. Our bodies will not betray us. They speak to us constantly, sending important messages – if we choose to listen.

If your body spoke English, it would say loudly and clearly, "Food is fuel for the body. Feed me when I tell you I am hungry". True body hunger (not the urges and cravings our minds send us) is a direct communication that your body needs fueling.

What are your body's true hunger signals? We're all different but some signals are pretty universal such as a growing emptiness in the belly, growling stomach, feeling shaky. I challenge you to become intimate with your hunger signals. That information will serve you well and teach you how your body talks to you. And by the way, visions of sugar plums (or chocolate chip cookies) are not hunger signals!

Here's a great analogy. True body hunger is like the gas tank in your car. As you drive, the tank sends you messages. The needle on the gauge moves from the full, to the empty position. At three-quarters of a tank, you don't need to pay attention. But as the needle moves toward empty or the gas pump symbol lights up, you'd better be asking, where/ when am I going to get my car it's next meal/ refueling. Same thing with our bodies. When they speak, when they send hunger signals, we need to refuel (for most of us, every three to five hours).

Take this metaphor a bit further. The last time you were at the gas station, did you see a "sugar-water" option at the pump? Silly question, of course, because we're smart enough to know that cars need (nutritious) gas, not sugar-water, to get them to run properly. So do our bodies! Sorry, but ice cream, cookies, and cupcakes are not proper fuel. Do they have a place in our lives? Absolutely, but not as means to energize our bodies and to allow our brains to think clearly.

Final part of the analogy. Please, please, please, stop trying to put gas in an already filled tank. How many times have we eaten everything on our plates or gone back for seconds, without feeling or thinking, how filled is my belly (tank) right now? If we slowed down for a few moments, what would our bodies say to us? Maybe we'd learn about our own "you've had enough" switch, similar to the one at the gas pump that automatically shuts off when the tank is full.

So… although there is no body magic, there is body wisdom that will lead us to health and well being, free us from obsessions with food, and will teach us a language that we will use for life. Listen to your body talk – and your car!

Ilene Leshinsky

Addicted to Food? Maybe Not

"I'm addicted to food." "I'm a foodaholic". I hear many of my clients express these beliefs and if the truth be told, I used to say the same things about myself. I remember planning binges that consisted of high fat, high sugar, and high salt foods. One of my favorite "meals" after a long, hard week in the retail industry (many years ago) was two huge chocolate chip cookies, an extra large bag of Doritos, and a two-liter bottle of Tab (I said it was a long time ago). Can anyone find any protein in those choices? After eating all of that, or two large tacos, two orders of large onion rings, and two large cookies (yup, chocolate chip), I'd feel like I was in a fat and sugar induced coma. Soon afterwards I'd fall asleep and wake up the next morning with a food hangover. Many of you know exactly what I'm talking about. Been there, done that, you're thinking.

There's actually science behind that physiological response. High fat and sugar foods activate the pleasure centers in the brain, producing dopamine, in similar ways that alcohol and drugs affect the brain. And the more pleasure we experience, the more we want. Right? Well, kind of. Just like brain altering chemicals eventually affect quality of life (an understatement), high fat and sugar foods and the impulse/ compulsion to eat more of them, can lead to obesity and numerous life threatening illnesses.

Okay, so now what? Do we throw up our hands and say not my fault, my brain (the devil) made me do it? A resounding NO! We go back to basics. Our bodies have innate wisdom. They signal us when we're hungry and when they do, they want nutritious foods that will fuel both body and brain - proteins, complex carbs, fruits, veggies, dairy products (so many of these are delicious, so stop thinking BORING) – not high fat and sugar choices that make us lethargic, put us in metabolic crisis, and cause us to crave more high fat and high sugar foods. If you want to explore the science behind the cravings, read <u>The End to Overeating</u> by David A. Kessler, MD, former FDA commissioner and self-proclaimed (recovering) overeater.

Our bodies are self-regulating machines so to speak. They need "fuel" every three to five hours and will send us signals when we need to "refuel" them. So if you're wondering if you're truly hungry, pay attention to hunger signals, (they often make noise in our bellies) and to the last time you ate. If you had a steak dinner an hour ago, you're not hungry!

So many of my clients feel like failures regarding their relationship with food. "Why can't I just shut my mouth and stop eating? Why don't I have any will power?" Here's where the similarity between substance addiction and overeating breaks down. Alcoholics and addicts can design meaningful, fulfilling lives, without using drugs and alcohol. We can't do that with food. We need food to live. And to complicate our challenge, right from birth, we were given food for both nourishment and nurturing. Of course we associate food and eating with comfort and connection!

I love food and I love to eat. Eating is one of the most pleasurable experiences in my life. However, just as recovering alcoholics decide to acknowledge their addiction and take responsibility for their behaviors, those of us who have food issues need to recognize our areas of vulnerability, our trigger foods, and take responsibility for our behaviors. I can't keep chocolate chip cookies or ice cream in my house but I can go out for a cookie or a cone! If we eat when we're not hungry and eat so much that we've made ourselves sick, we need to look at what is driving that behavior. What areas of our lives need fixing? What relationships need repairing? What are we procrastinating about and why? Why are we sad or angry and what can we do about it? If we're really being honest with ourselves, we know in our heart of hearts, that the answer is not simply "I'm addicted to food".

Ilene Leshinsky

Free at Last from Diet and Weight Obsessions

In her 1985 book, entitled "Making Peace with Food", Susan Kano chronicles her decision to feed her body, rather than starving it and to no longer focus on weight, size, and body obsessions. The book is part autobiography and part practical guide and is as relevant today as it was when she wrote it. She purports that most women in our culture have at least some traits of eating disorders, chronic preoccupations with food and weight, and behaviors that range from bingeing to semi-starvation. How could we not, living in our size 2 (or 0) obsessed world where all of the images we see in films, magazines and on television are of ultra-thin women and where every other commercial or advertisement is for a diet product?

Susan and I could be soul sisters. After a tortuous childhood as a fat kid and then years of dieting, I was finally thin, very thin. Like Susan I was obsessed with my size and weight. I prided myself on wearing the smallest size and weighing the least of all of my friends, acquaintances, co-workers, and most women in this country. I was pretty, petite, and obsessed, stepping on the scale at least five times a day and often dreaming of food.

One night, in one of my food dreams, a voice shouted at me, "Throw out your scale!" (I swear to you it was a dream not a hallucination.) So the next day I took my scale to the dumpster, and with more than a few moments of hesitation, I flung it in. Then I went to the grocery store to shop for "real food", promising myself that I would no longer eat fat free this and sugar free that. If Susan could do it, so could I.

What happened next was a process that paralleled Susan's. I made myself promises that I would eat whatever I wanted, that I would eat when I was hungry, and that I would stop when I was full. What I did not anticipate was how threatening this oh so natural approach would be. I got scared! So unbeknownst to my conscious mind, I started to play mind games. (You know them.) As the emptiness was growing in my tummy and the growling became louder, I would ask myself, "Am, I really hungry?" And then I would ask, "Do you really need to eat now?" The part of me still shackled to the past shouted a convincing no! What followed next was a prolonged struggle between mind and body, with my mind telling me to ignore my hunger signals and my body pushing me to respond to them.

Flash forward to the present. My relationship with food has stabilized. I follow all three guidelines for mindful eating and I exercise regularly. I'm strong and healthy and I'm free at last from weight, diet, and body image obsessions. No more mind games. No more pretending I'm not hungry when I really am. No more pretending I'm hungry when I'm really not. And yes, my body has changed. It's at natural weight and size. Do I weigh more than I used to? Yes. But I'm free (at last) from all of those obsessions that prevented me from fully living my life.

Want to join me? Here are five steps to freedom:

Let your body lead you. It will tell you when to eat and when to stop. (It's not your body that propels you to eat that whole half-gallon of ice cream.)

Talk gently and lovingly to yourself. Stop berating yourself and your body for imperfections. (We would never talk to another human being the way we talk to ourselves!)

Hang out with like-minded women who embrace that beauty comes in all shapes and sizes and can have a conversation that doesn't revolve around dieting.

Appreciate all that your body does for you. Value its functions – not just its form.

Love yourself for exactly who you are. Let go of comparisons to other women, their lives, their jobs, their partners, and their bodies.

Can you add to the freedom list?

Ilene Leshinsky

The Gifts of Menopause

Hot flashes. Night sweats. Vaginal dryness. Thinning pubic hair. Mental confusion. Increased depression, anxiety, and irritability. Slower metabolism. Thickening waistline. Weight gain. Thinning bones. Wrinkling skin. Decreased sex drive. Painful intercourse. Yes, these and more are the many "gifts" of menopause and I experienced most of them, all because of changing levels of the hormones estrogen, progesterone, androgen, and testosterone.

I thought I would sail through menopause. After all my years of healthy eating, regular exercise, good sleep hygiene, and caffeine monitoring, I figured "the change" would be a blip on my screen of life and no real change at all. Boy, was I wrong! At the time I was Clinic Coordinator at a county mental health clinic. I remember sitting in a staff meeting with sweat profusely pouring from my face and body – in the middle of winter. I remember how much I had to concentrate on a staff member's case presentation in order to retain the necessary information. How my brain felt like a sponge. I remember being awakened in the middle of the night by my body's inner thermostat that triggered rivers of sweat, soaking my nightclothes and my sheets. And the fatigue, oh the fatigue, from lack of sleep.

Silly me! I was going to do "it", "the change", differently than my mother had, without factoring in my genetic predisposition. So with a little medicinal help (yes, I went on hormone replacement therapy after having tried every tincture, supplement, and soy product on the market) my debilitating symptoms decreased significantly or went away entirely. As my wonderful gynecologist reminds me, "it's about quality of life, Ilene". And it was restored.

Interestingly, though, there have been other "gifts" of menopause, far more valuable than the diamond studs that I bought myself for my sixtieth birthday. In her important book, **The Wisdom of Menopause,** Dr. Christiane Northrup another postmenopausal woman and a OB-GYN, says, "the hormone-driven changes that effect the brain… give a woman a sharper eye for inequity… and a voice that insists on speaking up". This is a very different message than many of us heard and lived. Make nice. Keep the peace. Put others first. Go along to get along. Swallow your hurts. Look pretty. Those socio-cultural messages are harmful to the physical, emotional, and mental health of women, and become harder to tolerate in menopause. Like some of my clients, I had some soul-searching to do.

Not surprisingly, according to Northrup, I became increasingly discontent with my status quo. That dissatisfaction fueled my vision of opening a private psychotherapy practice for women of all ages. "Speak your truth", I often say to the women I work with. Yet in order to do that, we need to give ourselves permission to experience the messages that body, mind, and spirit are sending. We need to pay attention to the bubbles of inspiration and the pinpricks of deflation that arise when something happens to us, when we read something, when something or someone wounds us or makes our hearts sing. These psycho-spiritual messages are harbingers of change, transformation, and healing. Some of us are paying attention and taking action. Others are still fearful of what is on the other side of change, which can be very scary – and also very exhilarating.

Today, we women are living well into our seventies, eighties, nineties, and beyond. Menopause, "the change" is truly that, an opportunity to make changes, to redesign the second half of our lives, to heal from the wounds of the past, to create, to inspire, to transform our lives, as well as the lives of the ones we love.

So many gifts – of menopause.

Ilene Leshinsky

Happy Is a Choice!

I was raised by parents who grew up in the aftermath of the Depression. Both felt the aftereffects of scarcity and fear, particularly my father. When I was very little I remember saying bedtime prayers with my mother and younger sister (my father was still at work) and asking God to please help Daddy get out of the hole. Where was this hole in the backyard, gone by the time the sun rose and why couldn't Daddy just climb out of it? I agonized about this every night. Of course now I know that my father had financial worries about expanding his business and "the hole" was a considerable amount of debt. I inherited his psychic fears and anxieties.

But as a child of the "boomer" generation, I also remember many things in excess - clothing, antiques, cars, and of course food. Three refrigerators and two freezers held enough food to feed three armies with one mini-frig stocked with nothing but chocolate. Just great for a sneak eating, overweight child who was just too emotional, or so she was told.

Anyway, between post-depression era anxiety, intergenerational depression, and the trials and tribulations of everyday family life, home was not a comfortable place for me. Don't get me wrong, my parents did the best they could, but I was and still am one of those sensitive types, who absorbs the emotional vibrations of others – and I absorbed it all.

My family legacy and genetic inheritance did not make me by nature "a happy camper". However, I had best friends who welcomed me into their homes that were filled with love and laughter. And going to college in Boston provided me with distance and a respite from family struggles. I smiled more and I ate less.

After healing from an unhappy and unhealthy first marriage and I won't tell you how many years of psychotherapy (no wonder I became a therapist!), I learned some important truths about myself: I can feel happy. I can count on myself for my own happiness.

And… I have to work at being happy.

As I mentioned earlier, I'm extremely sensitive to the energies of those around me, as well as to my own. So now when I feel myself going down into the valley of anxiety or depression, where my thoughts are not helpful to my mental, emotional, or physical health, I have to put on the brakes. I have to change the direction of my thoughts. Entertaining them only leads to ruminating about problems, issues, and wounds both past and present. When I don't catch the thoughts soon enough, I can literally feel the energy draining from my body.

So over the years, I've paid attention to the things that lift my mood and make me smile. One of the things that drew me to my second and forever husband was his light and bright energy. Also, his willingness to play, and his sincere desire to understand me were high on my list. Being with my husband makes me happy! Walking with him and our dog Roxie each morning makes me smile. Feeling the rewards of the work that I do makes me happy. A good night's sleep makes me happy. Reading a good book, taking an afternoon nap, eating good food, visiting Florida in the winter to escape the cold – these simple things make me happy. And how can I not mention my weekly dish of ice cream. Ice cream makes me very happy!

So what do I do when I feel my life force, my "chi", start to drain from my body or when it feels like an elephant's foot is on my chest? I stop. I take a deep, cleansing breath in and exhale out the negative energy that's bringing me down. I ask my husband for a hug and I absolutely do not let those thoughts and resulting feelings take up residence in my mind or in my heart.

And sometimes I eat ice cream. I choose to be happy!

Ilene Leshinsky

Chapter 4:
It's Not Selfish... It's Self-love!

I remember the day I said to my husband, "I'm so jealous of you. You have time for anything you want to do!" He turned to me and asked, "If I can, why can't you?" His answer annoyed me. I'm thinking... he doesn't have to do this and this and this or that before he has to go off to work.

We women often, if not always, do everything for everyone else before we do anything for ourselves. We've been trained—by our mothers and their mothers—to take care of everyone else first. And then what happens? We run out of "day" before it's our turn. This often happened to me and so many of my clients.

And we wonder why we're wandering the kitchen at midnight, looking for something to eat, telling ourselves we're hungry, when what we are really saying is: **It's finally my turn!**

So, I started getting up about twenty to thirty minutes earlier than usual. With a cup of coffee in hand, back then my gift of self-love was to read a novel. Over time I realized that I was starting my day with a gift for myself. And, in one form or another, I am still doing just that! I start my day with self-love.

This chapter explores how we can incorporate self-love into our lives – and rethink the definition of selfish.

Ilene Leshinsky

Be Thine Own Valentine
Some Musings on Love

It's February and love is in the air. And candy and roses and sparkly pink and red greeting cards, along with romantic dinners for two and hotel rooms with petals strewn on their heart-shaped beds (I must have been watching too many "Sex and the City" reruns). For so many women there's so much pressure to find a date or be asked on a date for Valentine's Day. For many, many other women, the day is filled with sadness and loneliness.

My husband and I have been married for twenty-three years. And every day is Valentine's Day! Well, yes – and no! Yes, because I continue to feel blessed with his presence in my life. Every day I am grateful that we both said yes so many years ago. And no, because not every day is filled with romance and flowers and chocolate. (Thank goodness! All those calories consumed in non-fuel foods!) I love that he has enhanced my life and my journey… but he has not defined my journey, either. And, staying connected has been a lot of work – meaningful work, but work nonetheless.

I spent fifteen years in between husband #1 and forever husband #2. In the beginning, after my divorce, holidays, all holidays, were brutal reminders that I was alone. Not to say that I didn't have a "date" on any of those fifteen Valentine's Days. But I don't remember any special ones – until I decided to become my own Valentine, my own Ms. Right. One year I bought myself a card and flowers, another year a box of chocolates (a big mistake in that I ate the whole thing). One year I remember treating myself to an antique aquamarine (my birthstone) ring. And one year I gathered together my favorite women friends for a fancy dinner out. All of these outward expressions were a part of my inner journey to self-love, self-acceptance, and to becoming the woman I am today.

I was in Florida for two weeks in January. (Don't hate me. The average temperature was 72 degrees.) I had lunch with a woman, formerly from the Boston area, who I had not seen in twenty years. She's a full-time Floridian now. We know each other because many years ago, I introduced her and some of her friends to BodySense and we all worked together for over a year. After catching up, she talked about her divorce, a messy and painful one, and how her life has unfolded since. "I don't care if I ever go on another date", she shared, "or if I ever have another love of my life. I have **MANY** loves in my life now (and she listed children, grandchildren, other family members, dear friends, and colleagues) – and I'm one of them. I'm one of the loves of my life! And I love this journey that I'm on." As she said this to me, her face glowed, and so much love energy exuded from her. My Florida friend and I have learned to be our own Valentines.

I was watching a rerun of "Titanic" before the Patriots/ Broncos play-off game (boo hoo!) and a line delivered by Rose's mother caught my attention. Rose, Kate Winslet's character and the daughter, is bemoaning her fate of having to marry a wealthy but abusive man and she tells her mother that it's not fair. Her mother says (and I'm paraphrasing here) that of course it's not fair. We're women and we have few choices.

Wow! What a difference a century makes! In 1912, women had few choices as Rose's mother reminds her and us. In 2014, however, on this Valentine's Day, each of us has the choice to celebrate ourselves for who we are or who we are in the process of becoming, for our innate wisdom, for our beauty, both external and internal, for our accomplishments, and for our yet to be realized dreams. Each of us has the freedom to determine the direction of our lives.

Whether partnered or not, on this Valentine's Day, please do something special for yourself. That act is an affirmation of your value and worth - to yourself and to the world. And today and every day, please, be thine own Valentine!

Ilene Leshinsky

Learning to Be Number One!

This past winter I was watching a football game with my husband and the TV camera panned across the stadium. A whole section of fans raised large foam fists with extended index fingers and shouted "We're #1!" That moment got me thinking about what it means to be number one. Regarding what? To whom? What are the criteria? I remember being #1 in a spelling bee when I was in the fourth or fifth grade. And I was the shortest (and heaviest) girl in my second grade class. I guess that counts as #1 (although that's not on my resume).

Dear women readers, what does it mean to be number one? To put ourselves first on our "To Do" list. Do we make the top ten? Are we even on the list? Many of you are rolling your eyes now and thinking: Is she kidding? When is there time to think about me? To take care of me?

I struggle with this a lot! Balancing multiple priorities isn't easy. What happens if a client calls with a crisis and the only slot I have is during my lunch hour? How many nights do I work so that my working clients can be seen? It's the weekend, the list of house projects has doubled – and I'm pooped. And I don't even have children! Trying to fit in "me time" is even more challenging for parents with work, sports schedules, doctor's appointments, homework, and family mealtime (what's that, you ask?). One client recently quipped that she would put herself on her "To Do" list in 2020 when her youngest child turns eighteen and goes off to college.

So I ask you, can we mentally, emotionally, and physically wait that long? Dr. Christiane Northrup, MD presents the following scenario during her "Women's Bodies, Women's Wisdom" presentations: You're on an airplane, traveling with your young child in the seat next to you. The cabin pressure drops and the oxygen masks fall from the overhead compartment. What do you do? Invariably, my group members, without hesitation, state that they would put the mask on the child. (Buzzer sounds… Wrong answer!) The right answer, according to Northrup and I would agree, is to oxygenate yourself first – so that you can assist your more than likely struggling child and other passengers in the throes of a panic attack. Putting ourselves first can save lives!

Now let me link what we experience as our physically and emotionally depleted lives to our relationship with food. Have you ever found yourself wandering around the kitchen at midnight, rummaging through the cabinets, mindlessly eating, exhausted? Some would say and I would be one of them that this behavior is a way of saying... finally time for me! Often our relationship with food and our eating behaviors are symbolic of our unspoken and unconscious beliefs about our lives. Everyone else comes first. Others are more important than I am. As a woman, a wife, a mother, it is my job, my role to meet the needs of others before I meet my own. Please, please, please,

challenge those beliefs. Self-care is not the same as being selfish! As they say, "You can't get water from a dry well". And you can't get enthusiasm, focus, and zest from a depleted woman!

Each of us needs to adopt an "I'm Number One" belief and the behaviors that support that. What are the things that each of us can do to foster our own importance? For me, starting each day with a gift to myself has been transformational. Reading a novel for thirty minutes works for me. No matter how the rest of the day unfolds, I feel that I have treated myself specially. What would work for you? Planning a vacation? Getting a massage? Going for a walk? Digging your hands in the soil? Sitting in the sun? Going to the lake (even in meditation)? Breathing deeply? And if none of these appeals to you, why not buy a big foam fist with an extended index finger and walk around the house exclaiming, "I'm Number One!"

Ilene Leshinsky

The Biggest Winners!

My husband and I (and Roxie, our dog) walk downtown every weekend for exercise and to have a coffee and a bite to eat. Sunday, June 9th was no exception. I knew that "The Biggest Loser" was coming to town and participants would be running and walking by my house on route to the finish line. What I did not anticipate was the excitement and energy in the air with exercisers of all shapes and sizes proving that you don't have to be of a "skinny-minny" to be an athlete or on your way to being one. It was a joy to watch!

I must confess, though, that I don't like the name "The Biggest Loser". To me it sends mixed messages and provokes many questions. Before I lost all that weight, was I a loser? If I lose the most weight, am I a winner? How did I lose the weight? Is weight the be all and end all when it comes to health and well-being? Can I be healthy at any weight and size if I am taking good care of myself by eating, healthy nutritious foods, exercising regularly, sleeping 7-8 hours a night?

If you're a regular reader of this column you already know that I have issues with a culture that focuses on externals – beauty, weight, shape and size, often at the expense of health, both physical and mental. And you also know that I believe that any extreme plan of diet or exercise is short-lived and generally promotes weight gain in the long run. Who could maintain the focus and energy required at the "the ranch" and live in the real world?

Anyway, back to the event. I saw many people I know – friends, neighbors, clients – running, walking, or volunteering. It was a great day to be outside, and in the midst of so many health-minded people. It made me proud to live in the North Country.

I often hear some of my clients say that they are so ashamed of their bodies they don't want to leave their homes to exercise, to go to the gym, or to find an outside walking route. Some have even had insults hurled at them from car windows referencing their weight and size as they exercised. Shame on us as a society for our judgments and our derogatory comments! And let's be honest. How many of us have ever had the thought or asked ourselves or a friend, "Is my rear end as big as hers?" Proving what? That someone in the world is fatter than we are?

It's been said by many theorists and social commentators that "fatism", the discrimination against "fat" people, is the last remaining "ism". There are laws that protect people from religious, sexual, and political discrimination. No such protections for people who are "fat". We, as a society, have preconceived notions about the character and intelligence of people who are overweight, obese, or fat (whichever term one might use).

Contrast this to the morning of "The Biggest Loser" event. People of all shapes and sizes, runners, walkers, people with babies in strollers, being cheered along the race route and heartily applauded as they crossed the finish line. The pride and sense of accomplishment was palpable from participants and onlookers.

If I had "the power" I'd change the name of the TV franchise to "The Biggest Winners". Any of us who take control of our bodies and minds – all of us who make a commitment to daily self-care are truly winners – The Biggest Winners!

Ilene Leshinsky

No Wonder We Feel Bad about Our Bodies!

How can any of us have positive feelings about our bodies? Think about it. Whether we're 24, 44, or 64, we are bombarded with media messages spotlighting our flaws. From too much belly fat, to jiggly thighs, from thinning hair, to thinning eyelashes, from too many age spots on our faces, to too much nail fungus on our toes, from surgeries for breast enhancement or reduction, to implants for cheeks or chins, from Botox to anti-wrinkle creams, there is no way we can feel good about ourselves if we look at all of the products, programs, or services that are available to us to perfect our outer appearance (one perspective) – or to make us feel imperfect, flawed, or bad about the way we naturally look.

I was at a conference in California in early June, focusing on the empowerment of women and the facilitator, a gifted and beautiful woman of thirty-eight, addressed this issue and labeled it as a media conspiracy on a global level. I was struck by this pronouncement from a highly educated, and considerably younger woman than I, echoing my long-held belief that much of what we see in the media is designed to firstly sell lots of products and services and secondly, to keep us "in our place" by making us feel bad about ourselves and how we look.

As you've heard me say before, it's hard to run a company, create a work of art, write a book or a play, become an Olympic athlete, or to become whatever we desire or go wherever our dreams lead us, when we're starving ourselves, spending more time in the gym than at home, or emptying our bank accounts for lotions, creams, or cosmetic surgeries or procedures that promise happiness. It's a challenge to feel good about ourselves in the face of all of these images of perfection, which we know are not really perfection because of airbrushing and Photoshop or because of the age of the models. (My favorite is those age spot commercials promising flawless skin, where the women using the products are thirteen. Okay, maybe they're eighteen.)

Even if we were genetically blessed with a long, lean body (in my next life!), we women would still have to contend with the physical effects of the aging process. To illustrate, my husband and I were looking through our wedding album the other day. The first thing he said was, "Boy, were you skinny". I took a breath. The next thing he said was, "Why did I even like you back then". I exhaled. Those were the days when most everything that entered my mouth was reduced calorie something or fat free or no sugar something else – before I created **BodySense.** What I also noticed was the difference in my hair, which was so much thicker, without gray, and that my skin looked like, as they say, a baby's bottom. That was 22 years ago and again I took a deep breath.

There's a skin cream commercial that tells us to defy the aging process. Think about what that means. That there's something wrong with or bad about getting older? That we don't matter or count if we age? That if we're not 22 or 32, thin and beautiful with long, silky, frizz-free hair, that we're not smart and sexy? Worse yet, that we're invisible? My dream for all of us is to embrace the aging process, to embrace our lives each day, each moment, at each stage of our lives. Yes, the stages, as we get older, present challenges, but also so many, many gifts.

I truly believe (and not just because I'm 64) that there's something magnetizing, appealing, and sexy, about a woman of any age who takes good care of herself, who smiles vibrantly, who exudes her own unique form of feminine energy, and who speaks her heart and her mind. So rather than defying the aging process and searching for body and face perfection, maybe we women could embrace each stage and each moment of our lives, with all of their challenges and all of their rewards. Maybe we could learn to love our whole selves – body, mind, and spirit.

Ilene Leshinsky

"Tootsie" and "The Ugly Duckling"

Did you see the Dustin Hoffman video that surfaced in early July, in which he talks about his "epiphany" while preparing for his lead role in the movie "Tootsie"? The video went viral as they say, as Hoffman emotionally explores how he was "brainwashed" into seeing women primarily as objects of beauty. He tearfully states that throughout his life he missed out on knowing many interesting women. Why? Because they weren't attractive enough to catch his eye.

The premise of the movie, filmed in 1982: Out of work, difficult actor lands the role of an assertive, female hospital administrator on a daytime soap opera. While preparing for the movie, Hoffman wanted to see what he would look like made up as a woman. He wasn't satisfied, he said, with what he saw and wanted the make-up and costume artists to make him "beautiful", to which they responded – this is as good as it gets. The video got me thinking (again) about the plight of women in our culture.

I had a good friend when I was in junior high school. She lived across the street which is why we were friends because she went to private school while I attended public. Her family was rich. Mine was comfortable. However, we both thought we didn't measure up in the looks department. I was "fat" and she was "plain" or so we thought. But what I remember the most about my friend was her sense of humor. She made me laugh – belly laugh – and not much did in those days. And I remember her smile. It lit up a room – and yes, it made her beautiful. Would I have known this smart, funny, generous, kind and beautiful girl if we were not neighbors? The Hoffman video made me think about her – and the many opportunities we miss.

We miss out on beautifying our insides with so much focus on our outsides. We miss out on activities that could bring us joy and a sense of accomplishment because we're afraid others will judge our bodies. And we miss opportunities to have our lives enriched by some extraordinary people (men and women) because we don't give them a second glance. Why? Because they're not "pretty" or "handsome" enough?

In the fairytale "The Ugly Duckling", the baby swan was an outcast, abused, rejected, and abandoned by the family that she (yes, I changed the pronoun!) thought was supposed to love her. Not until she found her true family and her real home could she appreciate herself and the innate beauty that she had always possessed. There's a message here for all of us, I think. In a few of the feminist versions of the fairytale, the duckling's transformation occurs before she finds her swan family. She endures the trials of her early life and comes to the realization that she is a being of worth and value and beauty, even before meeting the swans.

In "Tootsie", Michael Dorsey, Dustin Hoffman's male character, shares that he believes he has become a better man as a result of being a woman. Firsthand, he learns about the objectification of women that many of us have had to endure. He learns about expressing and sharing feelings, about true heart to heart friendships, and about love and respect by being in relationships with women he is privileged enough to call friends.

Women give these things to the world. Isn't that enough to make us interesting ... and beautiful?

Ilene Leshinsky

The Long and Winding Road… to Self-Acceptance

I am 63 years old! Have I ever told you that? I realized that I seldom reveal my actual age these days. Not because of the stereotypical female thing – we lie about our age and our weight. And I never was that way when I was younger. In fact, I threw myself a fortieth birthday party and proudly announced when I turned fifty. I think lately it's been more about worrying that my younger clients and my students won't think I'm "cool" or "hip" or have anything relevant to share with them. And I think it also has a lot to do with the aging process itself and that my body has changed, along with my energy level. There are lines on my face and bumps on my body where at one time there were none. And also that socio-culturally, women in their sixties and beyond seem invisible (unless you're Hillary Clinton or Diane Keaton). So it dawned on me, as I've been writing recent articles about self-acceptance, that I'd better examine my own feelings.

In a recent article in **Psychology Today,** "The Path to Unconditional Self-Acceptance", Leon F. Seltzer, PhD notes that often self-acceptance and self-esteem are used interchangeably and explains the important difference between them. He says, "Whereas self-esteem refers specifically to how valuable, or worthwhile, we see ourselves, self-acceptance alludes to a far more global affirmation of self. When we're self-accepting, we're able to embrace all facets of ourselves – not just the "esteemable" parts. As such, self-acceptance is unconditional, free of any qualifications. We can recognize our weaknesses, limitations, and foibles, but this awareness in no way interferes with our ability to fully accept ourselves".

Wow! What a concept! To be able to look at ourselves honestly, warts and all, while glorying in our gifts and talents. To be able to accept our bodies, our aging selves, our humanness, without making a full-time job of striving for unattainable perfection.

Dr. Seltzer goes on to say that our ability to be self-accepting stems from our parents' ability (or inability) to communicate our okayness, beginning when we were newborns through age eight. No, this is not a blame the mother/ father indictment, but simply an acknowledgment that our ambivalent or negative feelings about ourselves often come from sources outside ourselves. What did we see reflected back to us when we gazed into the eyes of our parents when we were babies? What did they communicate about our being totally and unconditionally lovable? From my father, after eight years of trying to conceive me, I knew I was the "apple of his eye" and that of my "Bubbie", his mother. And I knew I was smart and could do anything I set my mind to. From both of my parents, I learned that my size was unacceptable and that the way I ate, inappropriate. The verbal and nonverbal messages were clear – and both have become parts of my personal legacy.

According to Carol Muter and Jane Hirschmann, in **When Women Stop Hating Their Bodies**, "The power to create an environment of self-acceptance is within you" (us). We can do that by developing within ourselves the "good mommy" who loves us unconditionally, as we try and fail and try again, as we get older, as we bump up against our limitations. They also remind us that when we go on diets to become acceptable, we often gain approval for not being ourselves. What a price to pay! What a Catch-22! And what a set up for disappointment and failure!

So what's the cure? Both Seltzer and Leshinsky would say that developing self-compassion goes a long way to growing the seeds of self-acceptance. One of the affirmations I still say is "I accept myself exactly as I am." Notice I did not say I will only accept myself when I have lost weight, toned my inner thighs, developed patience, and paid off my credit card debt. (You pick one or fill in the blank). And… self-acceptance does not mean our self- improvement journey is over. It's actually the first step in the change process.

I love this quote from noted psychologist, Carl Rogers. "The curious paradox is that when I accept myself just as I am, then I can change." Accepting ourselves as we are is the first step in developing our full potential – and in finding self-love. So… I accept my 63-year-old self exactly as I am!

Ilene Leshinsky

Let's Take Off Our Blinders, Please!

My husband brought home a book from the library in November and I read it, cover to cover in a week. "Willful Blindness" by Margaret Heffernan is a jolting exploration of why we turn a blind eye to the dangers that are right in front of us. Why, as individuals, communities, businesses, and countries we do not look at the obvious and why we keep trying to solve problems with methods that not only do not work – but often are harmful to us and our loved ones. The book is an eye-opener!

Reading "Willful Blindness" started me thinking about our fixation with the culture of thinness in this country – and its damaging effects. Look at these incongruities:

~ 95% of people (mostly women) who go on diets gain back their weight in one to five years. Yet we are constantly bombarded with ads and commercials for diet after diet, program after program touting the latest and greatest promise for weight loss and body sculpting. And, 95% of us are left with feelings of low self-esteem because we can't be successful with a process that is designed to fail.

~ 60% of women in this country wear a size 14 or larger. Yet when we turn on TV, open a magazine, or watch a movie, we only see women who are a size double 0 to size 2 – okay, maybe a size 4. Do we see ourselves in the mass media? What does being rendered invisible do to our self-image?

~ There has been a spike in eating disorders (anorexia, bulimia, and binge eating) in young (and not so young) women in the last ten years. Yet supermodels who weigh 23% less than the average American woman and whose BMI is on average 16.5 (well below the healthy range of 18.5 to 24.9) continue to be esteemed. And, models and celebrities on the covers of fashion and home magazines are photo-shopped and airbrushed to look taller, thinner, and "perfect". What does this teach young girls to value?

~ We have an obesity epidemic in this country. Yet gym, recess, and exercise periods have been limited or eliminated in many schools. The restaurant industry serves us enough food for a family of five – and we eat the whole thing! And… we choose to sit in front of the TV or go on Facebook rather than go out for a walk.

~ Little girls in the third and fourth grade, whose bones are still growing, are dieting and crying to their moms that they are fat!

What's wrong with this picture? How do we stop the madness? When will we take off the blinders and realize that the old solutions to our physical and mental health problems – through restrictive diets that tell us what we can and cannot eat, exercise programs that exhaust us, and magical thinking (you too can lose x amount of weight by drinking this tea or swallowing this pill) – are not working!

As we start the New Year and for many of us that start will include a resolution to eat less and exercise more in order to lose weight, can we frame it differently? Can we say to ourselves, or out loud to a loved one: This year I commit to health and well-being for myself and my family. This year I commit to eating when I'm hungry, fueling my body and brain with nutritious foods, eating slowly so that I know to stop eating when my body tells me it has had enough. This year I commit to moving my body regularly and being an exercise role model for my children. This year I commit to loving my body, respecting my body – not solely for how it looks – but for all the wonderful and miraculous things it does for me.

This year I commit to taking off my blinders, and letting go of magical thinking. This year I commit, by my actions, to creating a healthy culture for myself, my daughters, and for the next generation of women!

Ilene Leshinsky

"The Greatest Love of All"

Somewhere in the mid 1980's, during that fifteen year stretch in between husband #1 and my second and forever husband, the song "The Greatest Love of All " came out. It was popularized by Whitney Houston but my favorite version is the one by George Benson. The song is about learning to love one's self. I have this memory of trying to get to my office in downtown Boston, stuck in traffic on the Mass Pike with the song playing on the radio. Since I had nothing better to do (long before the days of smartphones and laptops), I really listened to the lyrics for the first time. It was Valentine's Day. I was alone and lonely and I started to cry.

Certain songs are markers in our lives, don't you think? I'm dating myself now, but junior high will always be linked to Neal Sedaka's "Breaking Up Is Hard to Do" and high school will always be about the Beach Boys. We remember the song we danced to when we met the love of our life. We choose songs for our weddings. (My husband and I chose Frank Sinatra's "The Best Is Yet to Come".) Songs mark our special moments.

Hearing "The Greatest Love of All", on Valentine's Day, when I was single, was a turning point in my life, a critical moment, a crossroad. I had an epiphany. I could follow the same path, the one I had been on for years, hoping that the next man, or the next clothing size down would bring me the happiness I was looking for. Or… I could take the other road, the one less traveled (to paraphrase Robert Frost) and start a love affair with myself. I chose the latter.

I have more than a few clients who insist that they will be able to love themselves only after they have lost ten, twenty, fifty pounds or a jean size or two. They believe that self-love will happen only after they are happy with what they see in the mirror or after finding the perfect partner. Fixing the outside, they believe, can heal the inside. They're wrong! And I tell them so, hopefully lovingly and gently. Actually it happens the other way around.

So how do we flip the switch? How do we learn to value what's on the inside, at least to the same degree that we value what's on the outside? How do we become our own Valentine? Here are a few tips:

~ **Take good care of yourself!** Get eight hours of sleep a night. Eat healthy nutritious foods. Exercise regularly. And make time for connections with loved ones and friends.

~ **Appreciate your body for what it does, not just for how it looks.** "Thank you, body, for digesting my food that gives me the energy I need to get me through my day."

~ **Practice random acts of kindness.** Do something kind for a stranger every day. The smile we get back will feed us much more meaningfully than ice cream or cookies.

~ **Affirmations are powerful.** Try one or more of these and say them ten times a day. (Remember, you're not supposed to believe these yet. If you did you wouldn't have to say them!) "I am lovable exactly as I am." "I am safe, protected, and loved." "My body is an expression of vibrant health and vitality."

~ **Find your gifts and talents and use them in the world.** Each of us has something special to contribute to others, to our communities.

~ **Act as if...** you are gorgeous, powerful, bright, creative, confident, kind and generous – right now. Imagine how these behaviors and soon-to-become beliefs would affect the way you walk into a room and how you are perceived by others and by yourself?

So let's all sing together... "the greatest love of all is happening to me. I found the greatest love of all inside of me. The greatest love of all is easy to achieve. Learning to love yourself is the greatest love of all." Happy Valentine's Day!

Ilene Leshinsky

A New Look at New Year's Resolutions

Wow, it's 2010! Is anyone besides me wondering what happened to 2009? Do any of us remember the resolutions we made at the beginning of last year? If you're like most people, by January 1st you had a list of resolutions that revolved around weight loss and exercise habits. And… if you're like most of us, by the end of the month, you probably gave up on them. (Raise your hand if you are one of us.)

So rather than waste time and energy on things we're not going to do anyway, I thought I'd offer a new look at New Year's Resolutions. How about making a commitment to just one – everyday, one day at a time. Here it is: Always Do Your Best. (Take a breath). I know, it sounds like a big deal, but read on.

In his extraordinary book "The Four Agreements: A Practical Guide to Personal Freedom", Don Miguel Ruiz informs us that your best will change from moment to moment. It will be different when you are healthy as opposed to sick, when you are rested as opposed to fatigued. Under any circumstances, he writes, simply do your best and you will avoid self-judgment, self-abuse, and regret. (Are you breathing yet?)

"Always Do Your Best" is the fourth agreement and according to Ruiz, the one that allows the other three (Be impeccable with your word. Don't take anything personally. Don't make assumptions.) to become deeply ingrained habits. I've read this book numerous times, suggested it to clients, and live the agreements myself (as best I can). So how does this fourth agreement apply to our connection with weight, eating, and body image?

As I go through my day, am I fueling my body with nutritious foods that will give me energy? Am I honoring my body with mindful choices? Am I eating my food slowly, thoroughly chewing each bite so that I enhance the digestive process? Am I able to recognize when my belly has had enough? Am I moving my body throughout the day and thanking it for all that it does for me? If I can't get to the gym, am I climbing stairs, dancing in the kitchen, jogging in place, power walking around my workplace? (Just so you know, the latest research states that exercising in ten minute bursts, three times a day, is as effective as a full, thirty minute workout!) As I go through my day, am I doing my best, knowing full well that I am not in control of where the field trip bus stops for lunch. I'm not in control of the weather, or if my child gets sick, or what my colleagues say to or about me, or if my partner remembered my birthday. However, I am in control of the choices I make and how I respond. I am in control of doing my best – to become healthier, kinder, wiser, and a better human being.

Always Do Your Best does not mean Always Be Perfect! That's a set up for failure. (We know who we are, those of us who go for a run with a fever, who push ourselves beyond pain and fatigue, who feel we're out of control if we eat a cookie.)

Always Do Your Best does not mean Always Let Yourself Off the Hook either. If a week goes by and we haven't moved our bodies at all and we're in good health, well just maybe we didn't do our best. If we berated our bodies all week because we don't look like Heidi Klum, we're probably not doing our best to talk to our bodies lovingly. (Fess up, you know who you are.) When we always do our best, we learn. We learn about our strengths, our limitations, we learn from our mistakes, and we learn about ourselves. We stop hiding from our humanness.

So this year, I resolve to always do my best. Are you with me?

Ilene Leshinsky

Lovin' Our Selfies

There was an interesting intersection of events that fueled the idea for this article – my 66th birthday, a mother and daughter "selfie" segment on the Today Show, and an event at Plattsburgh State at which I spoke entitled "Healthy Bodies, Healthy Minds".

I turned 66 years old in March. In service of full disclosure, I know I'm okay with my aging body. I know in my heart of hearts that I take good care of myself and at least to some degree, that self-care is reflected in the state of my health, my energy level, and in how I look. But – and this is a big but – I do wish that I were taller. No, I don't wish that I were a 5'10" tall Supermodel. Gone are those forty year old fantasies! But I do wish I could see a parade, breathe fresh air in a crowd, and not be mistaken for a child when I walk my dog. A few more inches, without heels, on this 5' frame would help. And don't they say that the taller one is the thinner one looks? Oops, did I really say that?

I was profoundly affected by the mother-daughter segment on the Today Show. Dove Products, in keeping with their promoting healthy body image in women and girls, sponsored an event in which mothers and daughters took selfies and then discussed their feelings about seeing their pictures. Many of the moms shared how they thought their daughters were beautiful – and smart. (Hurray, Moms!) The daughters, however, stated that they wished their moms felt the same way about themselves. They regularly heard their moms complain about their bodies being too fat or their faces too wrinkled.

Daughters wondered how they could believe their moms when these beautiful women (from the daughters' perspective) repeatedly bashed themselves about the way they look. The Lesson: daughters pick up on the subtle and not so subtle messages that moms convey.

One mother in the Dove segment was filmed applying makeup to her daughter's face and telling her daughter that makeup would make her look prettier – better. The daughter, who did not want to wear makeup, tells the camera and her mom that she wonders if mom doesn't feel that she is good enough without makeup – exactly as she is. To mom's credit, she recognized the negative consequences of her messages and linked them to ones she received from own childhood.

At the Plattsburgh State event, former model, now educator, writer, and filmmaker, Jean Kilbourne, via the Youtube video, "Killing Us Softly", explored the advertising messages, with which we are inundated daily, that depict women and girls in both sexualized and objectified ways. Aside from making us feel bad about our bodies without the "magic" of airbrushing and photoshop, these images have turned our focus from what we women can accomplish and how we can better our communities, to how we look - from what we can do with our lives, to how we can be sexier and better looking for our men. If you and I have personally rejected these messages (and I hope we have), well, the advertising industry certainly has not! And they are banking on young women and girls absorbing their images, and buying their products. And most disturbing, Kilbourne presents the link between the objectification of women – and violence against women. It's a lot easier to destroy, abuse, or kill an object than a human being, she reports.

So what's a woman to do? It seems to me that we have choices. We can buy into the messages that the advertising industry sends us. If we do, we'll be haunted by images of young, ultra-thin perfection that have been air-brushed and photoshopped, which are designed by the industry to make us feel bad about ourselves so that we will buy the products being advertised. Or... we can spiral into a depression because we'll never measure up to a standard of perfection that wasn't even real in the first place. Or... we can learn to love our selfies – ourselves.

And how do we learn to love ourselves? By taking good care of ourselves. By getting enough sleep, by eating healthy foods that fuel our brains and bodies, by exercising regularly for health and well-being – not solely with weight loss as a goal. And by hanging out with people who make us laugh, who feel good about themselves, and who are optimistic about life and its possibilities.

So I'm off to take a "selfie" on my smart phone that is still smarter than I am. But I'm catching up!

The Aging Goddess... Me

I turned sixty-five on March 2nd. Wow! How did it happen? Wasn't it just yesterday that my husband and I moved to Plattsburgh when I was forty-nine? And didn't I meet him just the other day when I was forty-one?

What I remember most vividly is how harshly I talked to myself about my weight, my size, and the shape of my body. I spent over half of my life berating my body, being verbally and emotionally abusive to myself. What wasted energy! And all of those negative messages I was sending to myself – that my body was absorbing. How I thought about her, my body, as my enemy, as something alien to me, as something to be whipped into shape. It makes me so sad now to think of the years I spent critiquing her, criticizing her, wanting her to be something she was not designed to be. I apologize to her and to my younger selves often. How confused I was about the true essence of beauty.

A few months ago, I was sitting with a client who has had weight and size struggles for much of her life. She brought in pictures of her younger selves for us to look at together. She remembered feeling so large and thinking she looked fat in all of those life stages that the photos represented. "I was so NOT fat," she said while looking at the pictures. "And "look at how cute!"

I remember seeing pictures of my former selves and having similar feelings of being too large and therefore unattractive. In one, I'm fourteen and sitting in a group photo with my cabin-mates at a summer camp in the Catskills. I looked happy – and if not thin – then certainly average – and cute! But at the time I believed I was so fat and I saw my adolescent self as so unappealing.

In another photo, I'm forty-three and sitting on a rock at Lake Willoughby in Vermont. My hair looked glorious, thick and wavy and half way down my back. However, I so clearly remember how much I hated my hair then – too wild, too frizzy, and never straight enough. Maybe one of the many gifts of the aging process is to appreciate, to be grateful for what we have each moment – in that very moment.

I look back fondly on the time in my life that I started to exercise regularly. It began when I rescued my dog Sammy from a shelter. And yes, initially I wanted to lose weight and change the shape of my body. However, as I moved my body regularly (and Sammy moved his) I discovered that I absolutely loved moving my body. We walked, we jogged and what started out as a desire to change my body's shape ended up as a mind, body, and spirit transformation. Even now, with some arthritis in my knees and hips, I love, love, love to move my body. And what a wonderful way, I discovered, to decrease anxiety and to increase mood!

You know those "old people" who wax philosophical about "if I only knew then what I know now"? Well, I've become one of them! I wish I knew then what a waste of time, energy, and money it was to focus for so many years on my exterior self – with only minimal regard for how I was ignoring my inner, emotional self. My older, Aging Goddess self would say to my younger selves, "Love yourself right now, for everything that you are. Love your body for all that it does for you. Love it for being the container of your soul. And love and nurture your emotional self. If you pay attention, it will guide you to your passions, to bring them to fruition, and to the capacity for great love".

Happy Birthday to me – and to all March Goddesses of all ages!

Chapter 5:
More Reflections... on Culture, Society, Men, and Aging

I remember writing the article titled "What I Learned When I Was Single" and experiencing feelings of both pain and joy. That article documented the fifteen years I spent single, in between my divorce from Husband #1 and meeting Forever Husband #2. Even the things that we feel will crush our hearts become our greatest gifts and our most important teachers!

Here is a potpourri of my thoughts and musings – anything and everything that crossed my mind or stayed in my heart throughout those seven years of writing for *Jill*.

I learned so much while researching and writing these articles. I hope that you find something that resonates with you in this last chapter.

Ilene Leshinsky

Therapy – It Works and It's Work!

I was 28 years old, living in a studio on Beacon Street in Boston, divorced for four years and miserable. I cried in the shower every morning, struggled to go to work, I couldn't do the dishes, take out the garbage, or make my bed. I lost my appetite (do you believe it?), slept fitfully, and watched my plants die because I didn't have the energy to water them. A dear friend of mine, a social work student, doing an internship at Beth Israel Hospital, said to me, "Ilene, you're depressed! Call this therapist friend of mine". I did. And that one call changed my life.

According to an article in **Psychotherapy Networker** (November/ December 2012), only 3% of Americans use psychotherapy or counseling services in a given year. Yet, the National Institute of Mental Health (NIMH) states that one in every five Americans (or 20%) has a mental illness at any moment in time. So why are only 3% of us getting counseling?

I remember my parents' reaction to my sharing that I was seeing a therapist. "You don't need that! We don't talk about problems with strangers! We don't air our dirty laundry in public! And when did you ever make your bed?" They were responding to the then and present stigma that surrounds and has surrounded the issue of mental illness for eons. 20% of Americans have mental health issues but only 3% are in counseling? What's wrong with this picture?

My clients tell me how long it took them to pick up the phone to call me - a week, a month, six months, close to a year in some cases. And when they finally do, universally, they experience a sense of relief. "Finally I'm doing something to take care of myself, to lighten my load." I felt the same way. But stigma and fear of being perceived as "crazy" often gets in the way.

We live in a complicated, demanding, and complex world. The issues my clients bring to therapy reflect this: unhappy relationships, struggles with parenting, balancing the demands of work and home, substance abuse, sexual abuse, domestic violence, eating disorders, why we use any substance (including food) or activity to distract us from our pain, our shame, our fear, our sadness – in addition to the possible genetic predisposition to depression, anxiety, or any other mental illness.

What I've learned from both sides of the couch (so to speak) is that therapy works – it helps us to feel so not alone. The best therapists nurture us, educate us, coach us, and bear witness to our pain. And… therapy is work! I had to be willing to reveal the real me – the good, the bad, the beautiful, and the ugly. I had to be willing to learn about me, to sit with "my stuff" to think and behave differently, to change. I was blessed with two therapists over the years who each created an environment where I was seen, heard, able to speak my truth, and not judged.

Some of my clients tell me that they have been on psychotropic medication (the kind that affects mood and anxiety) for a period of time before coming to counseling. They have realized that medication alone is not enough to help them transform their lives. Yet according to **Psychotherapy Networker**, the national trend shows medication use becoming the sole source of mental health treatment. (We've all seen the preponderance of ads for antidepressants). Yes, medication is helpful – and for some, necessary for stable mood and functioning. However, medication alone does not teach us how to be meaningfully connected to ourselves, our loved ones, our work. Counseling can and does!

So in this new month, of this New Year, many people will join a gym or exercise program to reshape their bodies. Some of us might enter into therapy to help us reshape our lives.

Ilene Leshinsky

Are Men Really from Mars?

There's a commercial on TV for a phone company where a male interviewer asks a group of young boys and girls if it's better to be faster or slower. Immediately they shout out in unison, "Faster!" Then one little girl elaborates by saying that if you're not fast you might be caught by a werewolf and then turned into a werewolf and then you'd have to stay at home and then you'd say "rugh, rugh, rugh" which means (she says) "I wish I was human again". And the interviewer, looking at her throughout the story with confusion says, "What?" This ad so reminds me of one of the major differences between men and women. (Don't be alarmed female readers, I am **NOT** comparing us to a five year old girl child.)

Many of the men in my life, since I've been writing my monthly Jill article, have asked why I don't address them – their male issues or perspectives. So here's my attempt at what I see are some of the differences between men and women that are both problematic and wonderful.

Back to the commercial about the werewolf and the phone company... She, the little girl, is telling a story to answer the interview's question and he's not getting what her story has to with his question. Ever come across this with the men in your life? We're telling a story to illustrate a point and their eyes have glazed over and they're yawning.

Important difference #1: Women speak in stories, with details, with tangents and turns. And men speak in headlines. I realized this early into my relationship with my forever husband. I'm telling him about something upsetting that had happened at work, and he's fingering his cuticles, and shuffling his feet back and forth. Master communicator that I am, I shared that it didn't seem that he was interested in my story. He told me that he didn't get the point, couldn't follow me, and what did I want him to do?

Important difference #2: Men want to fix things (including the emotional wounds of their women) and women just want to be heard with an empathetic and compassionate ear. So now when I want to talk about something I'm feeling, I preface my "story" with my need to share what I'm going through and that I just want him to listen. There's nothing to fix.

Many of the couples I work with come to me saying, "We just can't communicate. We have communication issues". And just as in John Gray's classic book "Men are from Mars, Women are from Venus", they feel they are from different planets, speaking different languages.

Important difference #3: Women tend to be more intuitive and effective communicators than men, talking through issues and using more non-verbal cues such as tone, emotion, and empathy. Men tend to be more task- oriented and less talkative. I remember many times early in our relationship when I believed how I was feeling came through my body language and my tone of voice but my husband was not picking up on my non-verbal cues. I've learned over the years to more directly share how I'm feeling rather than wish and hope and pray that he will intuit my emotional needs.

Here are two more big differences between men and women according to www.mastersofhealthcare.com:

~ Men's brains are 11-12% bigger than women's brains, which (sorry guys) has nothing to do with intelligence but explains the difference in their physical size and muscle mass (and why men lose weight more easily than women).

~ And surprise, surprise, women speak about 7,000 words a day while men speak about 2,000 (which brings us right back to importance difference #1)!

So why talk about this stuff. Long gone are the days of the 1960's when women proclaimed men and women were the same. We have fifty plus years of science and brain research to show us how wrong we were. And although differences can get in the way of easy communication, with patience, those differences can promote more effective, loving, and spicy partnerships.

Viva la difference!

Ilene Leshinsky

On Being Ken

"It's just as hard to be Ken as it is to be Barbie". A bare-chested young man, probably in his early 20's holds a sign with this quote on it. I found this picture on-line in the midst of numerous images of cut, chiseled, ripped, and buff men with six pack abs and well-defined biceps and pectoral muscles. Welcome to our world, guys, the world of impossible standards of beauty!

What's happening to men now has been the reality of women for decades. And as a result, we see a rise in eating disorders in men, particularly adolescents, displaying nearly the same symptoms as women. Male incidences of eating disorders are about 10% of all cases.

We all know by now that if Barbie were actually a real woman, she wouldn't be able to stand up due to the exaggerated size of her bust compared to her tiny waist and feet. Well interestingly, according to teen health.about.com, in the past twenty years, action figures, such as G.I. Joe have become more muscular, with their muscles more defined. And – just like Barbie – if Joe were a real-life person, it would be impossible for him to have the same proportions.

About five years ago, I was asked to be a consultant for a health and wellness program at a local gym. For a few weeks I would talk about BodySense principles to the women in the group. But I remember clearly the lone male participant during one round of meetings who was there to support his female relative. Eventually he shared how challenging it was for him to compare and contrast himself with many gym members who, from his perspective, were having much more success at sculpting their bodies than he was. His self-esteem was down and his anxiety was heightened as a result. Sound familiar?

So men have now entered our world. The National Eating Disorders Association estimates that thirty million people in this country have an eating disorder at some point in their lives. And the National Association for Anorexia Nervosa and Associated disorders estimates that ten to fifteen percent of people with anorexia or bulimia are male. Many experts however think that this is an underestimate, with the real number more like thirty percent. And with eating disorders having the highest death rate of any psychological illness, we now see boys and men participating in an already existing health crisis.

Part of the problem is that some (many?) medical professionals still see anorexia as "a girl's disease", according to Emily Alpert of the LA Times. So now it is equally as challenging to get a correct diagnosis if you're the mom of a male child, as the mom of a female child!

And what are the causes of the growing body image dissatisfaction (and its resulting eating disorders) in males? Most of the latest research suggests that just as with females, the media is the cause – or at least the main one. An article in the Harvard University Gazette looked at the differences in males from the West (the US and Europe) versus males from Asian countries. In Asian culture, where the intellect is highly valued, males were more satisfied with their bodies, and had lower uses of anabolic steroids compared to males in the West. Will that change as the standards of Western attractiveness continue to infiltrate Eastern culture? If what has happened to women across the globe is any indication, the answer is yes.

Hugh Jackman as Wolverine in the X-Men movies and Henry Cavill as the latest Superman know they are depicting fictional characters and realize that pushing their bodies to the limit is part of their job, for which they get paid millions of dollars. And they know their extreme measures are temporary, not a way of life. We women know only too well about the trap – the trap of believing that a beautiful body equals a beautiful and happy life. Only too well, we know it doesn't! Therefore, it's so very important that this harmful message is not passed on to males – particularly boys and adolescents - who should be striving to build their character – not just their bodies.

Ilene Leshinsky

Real Men Love Real Women

One of the reasons I love my husband so much is that he thinks most of the models in the Victoria Secret catalogues are "too skinny". Yes, that's a direct quote and boy, am I glad, since at five feet tall and a size 8 petite, I'll never make the front cover – nor the inside pages for that matter. I'm blessed with a man who has loved my curves and my aging self for over 20 years.

But what do most men like in their women? This question has cropped up often in my private practice. I sit with beautiful, intelligent women who feel undesirable, less than, unlovable, because they are not the shape and size they think men want. And by the way, most of their men love them just the way they are. They've told me so!

I've been reading a lot of blogs lately to research this article and this is what I found. Some men do like ultra-thin women. Some men like round, curvy ones. What most men like is a woman who carries herself with confidence, who has a great smile and can make them laugh. I have a client whose husband remarked to her that when she eats nutritiously and exercises regularly, she stands tall and confidently and flashes her beautiful smile to all around her. He finds this wife very appealing. However, when she eats "junk", stuffs herself to sickness, and doesn't move her body, she slouches, and avoids eye contact with him and others. This wife, he says, is not so attractive. Her weight and size are the same but her attitude is different.

You might find this interesting. Cosmopolitan Magazine did a survey in 2004 asking men what their favorite female body type was. 61.6% answered curvy with a large rack (their language, not mine). 20.4% answered svelte with big breasts, 11.6% stated model thin with small breasts, 4.7% said other, and 1.7% responded big and bodacious. So maybe not all men want us to be a size double 0 – 2?

Here are some representative quotes from the blog Ask a Dude:

"Real men want real women." "Guys are focusing on your weight because that's what you're focusing on." "There's nothing sexier to a man than a girl with confidence." "Big girls are just more fun to cuddle." "Health is sexy." So what's our problem? If so many men are accepting of so many body types, are we the problem? Yes – and no!

Yes, we have been brainwashed by media representations of airbrushed and photo-shopped images that tell us that a size 8 is plus size. So we diet relentlessly and pour ourselves into skinny jeans in order to be attractive. And no. Since beauty is in the eye of the beholder, some men are more attracted to thin/ skinny women. Have they been brainwashed too? Maybe. Or maybe they just like what they like.

And yes, there are some men who complain about the bodies of their partners. Here's a fascinating theory for you. In the 1980's Carol Munter and Jane Hirschmann wrote "When Women Stop Hating Their Bodies", an important book of the attuned eating movement. They make a statement that has stayed with me for decades. Speaking of us women, they write, "Bad body thoughts are never about our bodies, and always about our lives." (A profound statement and a topic for another article.) But they also say about partners, "The bad body thoughts that men have about our bodies, are never about **OUR** bodies, and always about **THEIR** lives. What is it about these men's lives that need fixing? And oh so interesting that they have come to believe that they would be happier if our bodies were smaller in some places and bigger in others.

Most of us – women and men – just want to be loved and accepted for who we are and not just for what we look like. The essence of who we are is what makes us special and desirable. The qualities of loving kindness, compassion, empathy, and humor come in all shapes and sizes. Most men see this. Real men know this. So why don't we?

Ilene Leshinsky

What I Learned When I was Single

When I was twenty-four years old, I became a divorced woman. I had been married for four and a half years and in relationship with this man/ boy since I was eighteen. Getting divorced rocked my world, turned it upside down, pulled the rug out from under me, and knocked me on my tushy. All the old clichés applied. At the time, I was a middle school English teacher and I remember the head of the music department saying to me, "Look at you Ilene. You're pretty and smart. You'll be remarried in two years." Fifteen years, and many lessons later, I met my second and forever husband.

Here's what I learned in those fifteen years.

Give yourself permission to grieve: Ending a relationship, particularly a marriage, is life altering. It changes your perception of yourself and your place in the world. Do whatever you need to do to calm and soothe yourself (safely, please). At the time, I thought that talking about my divorce was a sign of weakness (Can you believe I became a therapist?) and as a result my grief process took longer. Talk, talk, talk to empathetic friends, family, and maybe to a counselor.

Take good care of yourself – physically, mentally, emotionally, and spiritually: The same principles of self-care apply whether we're single, divorced, or partnered. It still amazes me how my view of the world completely changes with a good night's sleep, healthy food in my belly, and coffee or lunch with a dear friend. I know this is challenging when we're in pain but so necessary in order to avoid isolation and depression. And…in the midst of emotional upheaval, it helps to look out at the lake or the mountains or the ocean and appreciate the beauty in the world.

Learn to love yourself and others: For twelve years of my single life, I lived with big, beautiful Sammy – my teacher, my guide, my dog. Sammy opened my heart and taught me how to love again. Find a way to open yourself. A dog works miracles. So do children, gardens, and good friends.

Don't expect someone else to complete your life: Fill your own holes – from the inside out. Be your own gardener. Dream your own dreams. I made the mistake of thinking that the perfect (or not so perfect) partner would make me feel whole and special. I had to learn to be my own perfect partner – or close to it!

Build a life worth living: Endings are exquisitely painful. And… after the initial shock, they give us an opportunity to take another look at ourselves, and how our lives have taken shape. Some of us reinvent ourselves. I did, by changing careers, going back to school, buying a condo by myself. Go within. Is there a seed of a dream that needs nurturing? Now might be the time. It was at the moment I could honestly say, "I like my life and I am happy" that I met my husband (walking my dog, by the way).

Don't settle for less than you deserve: You are special! You have gifts and talents that the world needs. Please don't let anything or anyone (including yourself) make you feel "less than". The next person who enters your life should recognize your uniqueness, your spark, treat you accordingly, and feel blessed by your presence.

And this last lesson comes with the perspective of time and distance…

Sometimes the biggest hurts are actually the greatest gifts: Thank you, Ex-husband!

Ilene Leshinsky

"Every Moment Presents a Choice"

I still have a vivid memory of the moment my first husband asked me to marry him. We were driving up Beacon Street in Boston, on our way home and we were fighting – again and as usual. In the middle of the turmoil he said, "Let's get married". I remember hearing a voice inside of me (that I now know as my wisdom place), quietly and then not so quietly say, "No! You can't marry him." But I did. I was twenty-one, hopeful, and lost, all at the same time.

In the world of Cognitive-Behavioral Therapy (CBT) that would be called a critical moment, the crucial moment right before heading down one path, rather than another. In a recent article by Guy Finley (Guy Finley's Life of Learning Foundation), he speaks of that unique point when the direction of the world is changed by a single act. He calls this "inflection", citing historic events such as the invasion of Pearl Harbor, the discovery of the atom bomb, and the tearing down of the Berlin Wall. One dictionary definition of inflection is "bending, a turning from a straight line.

Interestingly for me and for us, Guy Finley shares that not only does inflection relate to historic events, but "the same holds very much true when it comes to experiences and resulting change in direction of our individual lives". And even more interesting, he explores an example that so many of us have encountered.

We want to change our eating behaviors. We want to eat healthier. Habitually at 4:00 every day, he says, we eat a bag of potato chips. So when 4:00 comes we head for the chips. And then we remember the promise we made to ourselves to eat healthier snacks when we're hungry. This is CBT's critical moment or Finley's inflection point – the opportunity to make a new choice.

Yesterday morning I consciously decided not to dip my hand into the bag of raw cashews for a second time. I lived through the discomfort of what it would feel like to experience my imagined or real emptiness without the second handful. I survived. I was fine!

Last night, however, after a long and stressful day, I had a handful (not a bag) of potato chips for dessert. I'm still strengthening my inflection skills it seems.

Many of us are aware of that moment when the world could change, our worlds, anyway. When we could do something differently, say something else, eat healthier, or not eat at all. What prevents us from firstly being aware of that inflection point – and secondly, acting on it?

Here's one hypothesis. Maybe we feel that we don't have the power within us to change. Maybe we feel beaten down by the circumstances of our lives (or of that day) and we feel overwhelmed by even the thought of doing something differently. Even something small feels huge. So we miss the moment – the many moments – each and every day to take, as Robert Frost said, "the road less traveled".

It seems to me that awareness, mindful choices, or making use of inflection points are like muscles in our bodies. If we use them, we strengthen them. If we don't, they atrophy. And the good news is that to build strong inflection muscles, we don't have to do it perfectly. It counts that we were mindful enough to even think about not eating the chips – even though we did – or to eat only a handful rather than the whole bag. The more we're aware of the inflection moments, the more likely it is that we will make a different choice the next time. And… there will be a next time.

So twenty plus years ago, when my second and forever husband asked me to marry him, I was faced with another critical moment or inflection point. Although I responded with the same "yes", I was clearly aware that my heart was smiling.

Ilene Leshinsky

Learning to Be Happy

I have a client who says to me every now and again, "I wish I had your life. You always seem so happy." I smile and think about some of the "discussion" I have had with my husband or that the cost of medical attention for our animals is putting my vet in a higher tax bracket or how irritated I get with littlest of things. But I think I know what she means. I have an open face. I smile a lot, and I tend to have a positive, optimistic view of life. I wasn't always like this, however. Childhood set the stage for unhappiness and obesity. (I was prescribed diet pills in the fourth grade.) And I learned by watching my parents that life was a struggle.) I took this lesson into adolescence and early adulthood.

However, in my mid-thirties, after a failed marriage and some career disappointments, I started to explore what were then called "New Age" approaches to life. I developed affirmations and said them religiously. I creatively visualized the life I wanted to have. I made vision board collages with pictures and phrases that represented, to me, a life worth living. I look back now and realize that at that time I was making a decision, conscious or unconscious, to change my view of life, to turn my mind toward happiness and fulfillment. I was transforming my inner environment so that my outer one could manifest differently.

In 1995, Sarah Ban Breathnach wrote *Simple Abundance* in which she explored the little things that we can do each and every day to be happy. One of her exercises was to create a "gratitude list", to enumerate 10 things we are grateful for each day. Oprah popularized this practice and for a while, much of the female population of this country was doing daily gratitude lists. It's a worthwhile practice and takes only a few minutes to change our inner states. "I am grateful for the sunshine on my face; kisses from my dog; this morning's beautiful sunrise; the love of my husband…" Are any of us still making our lists?

So often we think about and dwell on all of the things in our lives that are bad, not right, that make us unhappy. Have you ever noticed how your body feels when you are immersed in the negative? Mine feels heavy, weighted down, and I feel depressed. In his book, *Peace Is Every Step: The Path of Mindfulness in Everyday Life*, Thich Nhat Hanh has a mindfulness meditation called, "What's Not Wrong?". In this three minute meditation he asks us to turn our minds to what's not wrong, or what's right in our lives, including the oft taken for granted, but life giving act of breathing. How revolutionary! To meditate on the simple, yet profound gifts that life offers us each day. My clients notice a marked change in their bodies after this meditation. They report feeling lighter (not so terrible for those of us with weight and body image issues), happier, and more optimistic. And... this is consistent with what we now know about what happens to the brain when we think happy thoughts, rather than negative ones.

"Is there a biological dimension to happiness?" asks one of the Harvard Medical School Special Health Reports on Positive Psychology (2009). Yes, states the report! Brain chemistry is changed by positive emotions. Researchers have known since the 1950's about the "pleasure center" in the brain and the associated brain chemicals of dopamine, a neurotransmitter, and the opiate-like endorphins (triggered by chocolate and exercise), both associated with feelings of happiness and serenity. PET scans and *fMRI* have allowed us to observe that positive and negative emotions activate different parts of the brain. So there is now scientific evidence underscoring the importance of changing our negative thoughts (which produce negative feelings and behaviors) into positive ones.

So I'm off for my run with my dog, during which time I will be saying my affirmations and being grateful for the sunshine on my face. And when I meet with my client later today and she remarks about wanting my life, I will say, "I have learned to be happy!"

Ilene Leshinsky

What's Not Wrong?
Another Look at Gratitude

"What's not wrong?" asks Thich Nhat Hanh, the Buddhist monk, in a mindfulness meditation. He states that we so often look at – and look for – what's wrong, that we lose sight of our gifts and blessings. He goes on to list the many ordinary and extraordinary things that are present in our lives when we simply open our eyes at the start of a new day: sunrise, warm breezes, autumn foliage, the eyes of a baby, the wet nose of a dog, sunflowers in the backyard. So many things to be thankful for!

I'm a recovering "worrier". It's part of my genetic inheritance. (Thank you, Dad!) I remember being very young and saying bedtime prayers with my mother and my sister while my father was still at work. Every night, before closing the prayer, we would implore God, "Please let Daddy get out of the hole". I found out much later that the plea to God was about helping my father make money at his newly created business. At five years old, however, I was looking for the hole in the back yard where I would find and rescue my father. No wonder I was riddled with financial insecurities for years.

As I'm writing this article, we are experiencing the first government shut down in seventeen years and I have my first cold in two. All the more reason for me and for any of us to ask the question, "What's not wrong". Through brain imaging we now know that thoughts and feelings have a dramatic impact on brain and body chemistry. Positive thoughts lead to positive feelings, increased mood, and an enhanced immune system. We also know that the opposite is true. Negative thoughts and feelings can negatively affect mood and anxiety, and significantly weaken our immune systems. You probably have experienced this yourself. Ever have a worry thought and chew on it and chew on it and chew on it (until all of its flavor is gone, as they say)? If someone were to hold up a mirror, you'd probably see reflected back to you, a scowling face and hunched posture. If you were to assess how you felt, you might notice heaviness in your chest or tension in your jaw, neck, or shoulders, and a deflation of energy. Worry makes me feel like there's an elephant's foot on my heart. What about you? Feeling joyous or down in the proverbial dumps?

And what a waste of time and energy! Does worrying about something real or imagined change the outcome? Absolutely not! If anything, worry spirals us down into the abyss of depression and anxiety, where it is nearly impossible to be at peace and to have serenity – and to climb out of the hole.

One of my clients went to a week-long mind, body, and spirit conference recently. One of the presenters, a medical and psychological professional, told the group that if we do just one thing, we can positively change our lives. Keep a daily gratitude journal, she said. Oprah popularized this concept in the 1990's based on a book by Sarah Ban Breadnach called "Simple Abundance". Listing five to ten things a day for which we are grateful can lift depression and decrease anxiety, bolster our immune system, erase scowl lines from our faces, and revitalize our outlook on our lives.

And no – our problems don't disappear. Having gratitude for our many gifts and blessings does not change the reality of a cancer diagnosis or a financial crisis. But boy, does it make those realities easier to face - and to handle. With gratitude in our hearts and finding "what's not wrong", every day can be Thanksgiving.

I'm off to do my list. Happy Thanksgiving, my sisters, today and every day! I am so grateful for you.

Ilene Leshinsky

The Female Prosperity Hormone...Oxytocin

Ever hear of Oxytocin? No, not the painkiller, oxycontin, but the hormone that is released in childbirth and assists in the bonding experience between mother and child. Well, more and more research is demonstrating that oxytocin is also the female prosperity hormone, and responsible for not only feelings of love and well being, but of increased collaboration and altruism in women - and in men. Interesting, don't you think?

In November 2011, I went to a four-day, women's conference in Los Angeles. Picture six hundred women of all ages, from all over the world, in a gigantic ballroom with incredible amounts of female energy filling the room. The event was sponsored by the Brave Heart Women organization, founded by the gifted and inspirational Ellie Drake, whose mission is to promote the personal, professional, and global empowerment of women. I don't even remember how I began receiving the emails from the Brave Heart community but the messages resonated deeply with me. So much of my work with women is about assisting them/ us with finding our truth and using our voices to speak that truth – in all areas of our lives. Ellie's message is similar.

If you lived through the women's movement of the 1960's, you saw many of us women operating in a male model, which required that we go out into the world and compete with men and our own gender. And many of us soon realized that operating like a man, and even looking like one, in business suits and tailored pants, did not feel comfortable or right for us. Tapping into the oxytocin hormone, that we naturally produce more than men, can help us change that model from competition (male) to collaboration (female). This is one of the underlying principles of Brave Heart Women.

Did you know that up until eight weeks old, the brain of a fetus is unisex? At eight weeks, however, in utero, the brain of a boy baby receives a rush of testosterone, which infuses the male with aggressive and procreating drives. And this will come as no surprise to many of us - the influx of testosterone shrinks the communication center in the male brain. For girl babies and the women we grow into, however, that communication center remains wide open! Ever wonder why we women pick up on subtle cues and men, well not so much? Now you know.

Baby girls, soon out of the womb, with wide open communication centers, scan their environment looking for cues from mom, through eye contact, body language, tone of voice, and the way we're held, that say, "I'm glad you're here. I want you in my life. I love you." That nonverbal communication releases oxytocin to both mother and baby. (Ever notice that when we give or get a really great hug, how our bodies seem to melt into that of the other and we feel a positive change in both brain and body chemistry? That's the oxytocin effect!)

However, if we didn't get enough, as we say in my world, of "unconditional, positive regard" from our caretaker(s), we learn to seek their approval by trying on different behaviors that will get us what we want and make us feel loved. Ellie would say that our need for approval is biologically ingrained in each of us and was necessary when our female ancestors lived in caves and trees and needed to trust that their men would come "home" with food and protection. However, she would also say that our need for approval is the number one, evolutionary obsolete behavior that we still engage in!

Every time we do not listen to the little voice in our wisdom place and everytime we behave in ways that are contrary to what we know is right and true for us, in order to gain approval, we kill off a part of ourselves. We sell our souls bit by bit. In our personal relationships, we develop a false self. In our business ones, we avoid taking risks.

So circling back to oxytocin... Unlike adrenalin that revs us up and puts us in fight, flight, or freeze mode (and stores fat in our bellies because of surges of cortisol), oxytocin allows us to embrace our fear and to take appropriate risks, which potentially enhances our prosperity, while we remain calm. So take an oxybreath with me now and you'll see what I mean. Inhale deeply. Hold it. And then on the exhale, with a feminine sound that starts at a higher tonal range, emit "haaaaaaaaaa", until you have no more breath. And if you really want to feel better, repeat that breath two more times.

And if you really, really want to feel better, oxybreathe eight times a day, and couple each breath with an oxyhug, a fifteen second hug that matches left side to left side – or heart to heart. That's expert advice from Dr. Paul Zak, a neuroeconomist and oxytocin researcher at Claremont Graduate University in Southern California, nicknamed Dr. Love by his employees, for giving oxyhugs regularly.

So yet again, we learn that women are different from men, with science backing up our intuitive knowing. To paraphrase the Dalai Lama, if the world is going to change, it is Western women who will propel that change. Ellie Drake and Paul Zak would add that a catalyst for women changing the world and ourselves will be oxytocin.

We're All in the Same Boat

In my office waiting room, I have an oil painting of a small rowboat adrift on the sea. The boat is empty, about to go under and the sea is turbulent. It was painted by a former client, a young woman who I met when she had been struggling with bulimia for seven years. She gave me that painting right before she successfully ended treatment. She said the painting depicted what life was like for her before treatment – all alone in the boat, unable to guide it through rough waters, unable to get her bearings – and how good it felt to finally have someone in the boat with her for guidance, support, and empathy.

How many of us have felt all alone in our struggles with food, weight, and body image? How many of us have felt like we were drowning all by ourselves? According to the latest data, 80% of us American women are in conflict.

At the end of October, I stood in front of a roomful of wonderful women to facilitate a one-day event on BodySense principles. Women of all ages, of all shapes and sizes, and with all kinds of eating issues attended. As I thanked everyone for coming, I was in awe of the courage in the room - my courage for planning and leading the retreat and their courage for identifying themselves with food and eating issues. It was a day filled with lots of laughter and learning.

Here's what we learned:

- **We are not alone!** So many of us have similar feelings about our relationship with food and with our bodies.

- **We often use food to comfort our emotional selves.** And since we are very smart, we are clearly aware that there are other calming and soothing alternatives but we eat when we're not hungry anyway.

- **We ignore our bodies and their signals.** We don't get enough sleep and exercise to sustain good health and we don't pay attention to our hunger signals so we become depleted (and grouchy – this one's me – just ask my husband).

- We eat too fast! As Dr. Oz would say, we "grab, gulp, and go". And we wonder why we eat too much and have acid reflux? (Picture your poor stomach trying to digest a whole piece of steak rather than a thoroughly chewed mouthful.)

- We categorize foods as good and bad. Lettuce is good. Cake is bad. And we feel guilty when we eat "bad" foods.

- We're all or nothing thinkers. If we don't have time for 30 minutes of exercise, we skip it for the day – 10 minutes is not good enough. If we eat a cookie, we've blown the day. But we'll be "good" tomorrow.

- We belonged to the "Clean Plate Club" as kids – and we still have our membership cards as adults. Time to tear them up, don't you think?

- We struggle to fit in when we feel different than what we see in the media – a different size or shape or lifestyle choice. How can we feel good about ourselves when we're not a size 2? How have our lives shrunk because we feel we're too fat?

- We are Wise Women! We give comfort and support to others by our physical presence and our words of wisdom and compassion.

- We are jugglers. The balancing act is challenging at best. It's difficult to juggle the care of others with care of self. When we drop the ball, it's usually the one with our name on it.

- And most importantly... we learned that we're all in the same boat! Forty women, from their 20's to 70's, of varying sizes and shapes, with different eating issues, learned that although we are different, we are the same.

And what a boat it is – filled with bright, brave, and beautiful women!

Be My (Supportive) Valentine!

In early December I asked my husband to purchase a platter of assorted fruit for a holiday luncheon at Plattsburgh State where I teach part time. He came home with the fruit – and a five-pound box of butter cookies, some with colored sprinkles, some with dollops of chocolate on top, and some with fruit centers. If you can't tell already, I have a thing for butter cookies. And, these melt in your mouth beauties, the size of fifty-cent pieces, were a hundred calories each! Butter cookies are one of my trigger foods - foods that when in my house in quantity – call to me, and keep calling until they're all eaten (by me) or banished to the garage or dumpster.

"I thought you could bring these to the party, too", he said. "Not helpful", I replied, "to bring one of my trigger foods into the house". "I didn't know", he responded.

Okay, what's fair is fair. After twenty years of being together, he knows about the chocolate chip cookies, the various gourmet ice creams, but (I'll give him the benefit of the doubt) not about the oh-so-tempting butter-filled treats.

So what's interesting about this real life scenario is that the idea for this article came from my husband. A few months ago he suggested that I write about what partners can do to support their women on their journey to (pick the ones that apply) lose weight, exercise regularly, stabilize their relationship with food, and feel better about their bodies. To be perfectly clear, Husband, bringing five pounds of any kind of high fat, high sugar goody into our home is NOT a show of support. And to be perfectly fair, he has been a very loving and supportive partner as I've journeyed to weight and body image stabilization.

Many of us women have taken this trip many times. We've lost weight. We've gained it back. And we've lost it again. We've been on this journey before - and what we often forget – so have our partners. They've been excited for us, disappointed for us (and maybe with us), and excited again. What we don't always appreciate is that our changes can be unsettling, anxiety provoking, scary, and downright inconvenient for them! "You're changing and I'm not sure I like it", they're thinking or feeling.

Many of my clients share that at some point they feel undermined by their partners. Éclairs appear on the kitchen table, requests are made for fettuccine alfredo for dinner or eggs benedict for breakfast. Or, they get "the look" when wanting to carve out time to go to the gym. I tell my clients what I've done in my own life. Talk! Talk gently and lovingly to your partner about what you need and what you're feeling. And ask! Ask what you can do to make your lifestyle changes more understandable (and palatable).

And it might help to show your partner the following Don't and Do's. And please let me know if any of these suggestions have been helpful.

PLEASE DON'T:

~ Monitor your partner's eating behaviors

~ Make critical comments such as:

"Should you be eating that?"

"Haven't you had enough?"

"Are you gaining weight?"

"When's the last time you went to the gym?"

~ Sabotage your partner by bringing her trigger foods home

~ Insist that she eat what you want and that she eat when she's not hungry

PLEASE DO:

~Ask your partner how you can help (and accept her answers)

~ Have conversations about:

grocery shopping and meal planning

eating out

scheduling exercise time

~ Give her positive feedback about her lifestyle changes

~ Monitor your own feelings about the changes she's making in the way she looks and acts, and talk to her about them

~ Appreciate that as she becomes stronger and healthier, she is ensuring a longer and happier life together

Ilene Leshinsky

My Prime Time Resolutions for 2016

Another year! Another set of New Year's resolutions! This is the time of year when we get to wipe the slate clean and start fresh. We can begin again with our hopes for weight loss, more exercise, eating no carbs or gluten free, or maybe some of us want to develop a workable budget. All worthy goals and all things in the past I've promised myself year after year after year after year.

Maybe it's my age. Maybe it's the aging process. Maybe it's what happens when we want to live more consciously. But my priorities have changed. Yes, I still want to be healthy, so I eat right (most of the time) and eat to "hara hachi bu" (the Okinawan way of eating to 80% full) – most of the time. And I still exercise every day. Not for weight loss or six pack abs but for healthy bones, a healthy heart, and the ability to move – to dance. I think I've finally given up the ghost of body beautiful for what really matters, body healthy. I want to feel comfortable in my own skin. And I want to have enough – enough love, comfort, resources, friendships, and happiness to feel content. So what kind of resolutions does this aging and evolving woman make this year?

Not too long ago, I was racing down the hallway of my office building on the way to the elevator. I was late. I flew by a woman who was moving much slower than I. As usual, I was in a hurry. When I got to the elevator (I know I should be taking the stairs) I stopped. I turned around and called down the hall, "Are you going up?" She nodded yes. So of course I waited for her, feeling the seconds ticking by. When she got into the elevator, she gave me the biggest smile and said, "Thank you! You just made my day." I smiled back, felt the warmth of that exchange, and realized that actually, she had just made my day. So resolution #1 in 2016, I want to be kinder. I want to practice kindness every day, to everyone, including to myself.

I have a client who just recently said to me, "I have absolutely no patience. I wasn't born with any". Boy, can I relate. Particularly when I was younger, I'd race around to get things done, jam too many activities or commitments into the course of an hour or a day. Sometimes "it", whatever it was, would go well and I'd feel super accomplished, and a little like SuperWoman. Often though, my desire or need to get things done now and quickly would get in the way of it being done well, or sadly would cause me to be rude or disrespectful to someone, who unbeknownst to her or him, just got in my way. I would invariably find myself in the slowest line at the bank or supermarket, grumbling to myself about the incompetence of the teller or the slowness of the cashier. Unfortunately, I'm sure that I communicated my feelings quite clearly by my nonverbals – the tone in my voice, the look on my face.

I remember a particular day at the bank. I was in line, and again had chosen the slowest one. I couldn't help but overhear the woman in back of me, grumble and grouse about the teller who was doing her best to handle a complicated transaction for the man at her window. As I watched the face of the teller become redder and redder – with shame and anger – I made a promise to myself, from that moment on, to practice patience. And since I'm a "sooner than later" kind of a girl (just ask my husband), patience is still on my list, resolution #2 for 2016.

When I was a little girl, my father, directly and indirectly, tried to teach me that the world was fair. That if I put forth the effort in whatever venture, I would get "it" back, that if I was a "good girl", the world and the people in it would reward me in kind. Well, my father was wrong. And I watched his unhappiness and dissatisfaction with his life grow, as I grew into adulthood. The world, the universe, I learned, is random. So if we are doing what we're doing for the payback or if we're behaving in certain ways with the expectation that we'll be treated the same way in return, then we're setting ourselves up for disappointment and sometimes despair. My divorce from my first husband highlighted this lesson.

After all of these years, I'm still working on acceptance, resolution #3 for 2016. Acceptance that the universe doesn't revolve around me, that people don't always treat me in ways I think I deserve. That sometimes those people let me down. That this wonderful and forever husband doesn't always do what I want

Ilene Leshinsky

him to. Acceptance is tough! But with acceptance comes freedom. Freedom to be the best person I can be without expectation of gain, without a promise or hope of a payoff or payback.

So in 2016, I resolve to practice more kindness, patience, and acceptance. And if all of my efforts bring me fewer wrinkles and a lower body mass index, I won't complain. Happy New Year!

Reflections of a Fat Girl

Redefining Aging

"My biological age is 35 and my wisdom age is 300." I heard this quote from Christiane Northrup, MD on a recent PBS special. I sat up straight. It made me think.

Part of her presentation, "Glorious Women Never Age", was directed at any of us, men or women of a certain age who are automatically thinking that aging means getting old and decrepit. Here are some interesting facts to challenge that belief:

~ In the 19th century, the age of retirement was 65. According to actuarial tables then, 65 was the average age of death. Today we live about 24 years longer!

~ Baby Boomers are the fastest growing segment of the population with buying power equal to none (even though advertisers have forgotten us except for those selling insurance for funeral expenses and "I'm falling and I can't get up" alert systems). We'll be the largest segment of the population by 2050.

~ Since we can live 20-30 years after the age of 65, retirement for many of us is not the end of working, but the beginning of redefining our careers or even reinventing our work and personal lives.

In her presentation, Northrup suggests that we "co-author" ourselves and the aging process. What are the messages that we send ourselves about getting older? What are our friends and family saying? Our communities? Our society? The media? She illustrates by telling the story of getting off a plane and witnessing a sea of black balloons being held by friends of another woman passenger who was celebrating her birthday. She had just turned 40! OMG, another 40-50 years of living as an old lady.

Are we talking ourselves into old age? Northrup recommends not identifying ourselves as a senior citizen, even for the discount, because it often changes people's perceptions of us. The message here is about what our messages – subtle and not so subtle – say to our brains and bodies on a cellular level. Does our birth certificate define our age or does our zest for life? Northrup tells the story of one of her elderly family members who went to the doctor complaining about pain in her right knee. The doctor asked her what she expected at her age. The woman retorted, "I expect my right knee to feel like my left one! Well good for her!

Can we get older without getting old? Can we age without getting aged? I watched Northrup bounce around the stage with such vitality and enthusiasm. She's my age, I think: 35 years biologically with 300 years of wisdom (I hope). I was impressed and proud. She's another woman – and there are many of us (and men) – who won't let our date of birth define who we are. Depak Chopra agrees and sends a similar message that our bodies don't break down as we age. Unlike our cars that inevitably need fixing or replacing, the cells in our bodies are regenerating all the time.

I get it. I'm a realist and right alongside being "the glass is half full" kind of a girl, I accept that I am aging. I see the signs on my face and in my body. My knees just won't bend as far down as the young female instructor on the exercise video that I watch. But that doesn't mean that I've stopped exercising! Or moisturizing!

"Compared to older people in the past, boomers will actually have a greater opportunity to live a youthful old age", write J. Walker Smith and Anne Clurman, senior executives at the Yankelovich consumer research firm, which coined the term "baby boomers". "Four decades of Yankelovich research" they write in their book *Generation Ageless* "has found one thing about boomers over and over again – an unwavering determination to not get old."

Where's my mini-skirt?

Love and Happiness – in Our Prime and by Our Design

When I was in graduate school, studying for my Master's Degree in Social Work, I clearly remember a video that was shown in my human development class. A then 85 year old woman was telling the story of her life. The camera showed her and a considerably younger man hiking through a beautiful countryside. She shared that she had lived an unhappily married life for over forty years but stayed with her husband, she said, because of the children and the life they had created together. And then he died. And then at 65 years old, she fell in love, deeply in love, for the first time in her life.

I met my second and forever husband when I was 41. He was 39 (but I looked younger). I met him after fifteen years of being single and as my friends used to tell me, after dating nearly every single man in Boston. After my first husband and I divorced, Mr. K., the music teacher at the Holliston Middle School where we both taught, said to me, "Don't worry, Ilene. Look at you. You're smart and pretty and you'll be remarried in two years". Well… two years plus thirteen later, my now husband saw me walking Sammy, the dog (he played a big part in our story) around Jamaica Pond on a beautiful spring day - and the rest as they say is history.

When I met my forever husband, I had reconciled myself to living single. And I had created a good life for myself and my animals. I bought a condo, had my own marketing business, and a number of close female friends. It was a good life and I was happy. And then bam – George ran into me at Jamaica Pond and life as I knew it changed. Back then I asked myself, "Can I be single and happy?" The answer was yes. And the answer is still yes, although I'm so glad that I have him and my coupled life, for so many reasons.

I've learned so much more about myself from being one half of a couple. I've learned how to be a better, kinder, and more compassionate human being. My life has been enriched by being married. And boy, has it also been stretched. Really stretched! How do two very different people negotiate differences – lots of differences - and remain kind and loving in both word and deed. We've been married for almost 25 years and we're still learning and growing and stretching.

A number of my friends are without a life partner – some from divorce and some never coupled long term. Each has a full and rich life – by her design. One winters in Florida and summers on Cape Cod. Another, when she's not working, travels all over the world – by herself. And they tell me they are happy. Sociologically speaking, they fall into the statistic that women have an easier time being single than men. We find other women to hang out with – at our workplaces, in the gym, volunteering, or doing artistic pursuits. We fill our lives with meaning and the data says we're happy – and happier than single men. My friends are testaments to that.

In a recent AARP Magazine article entitled "Single and Loving It", biological anthropologist, Helen Fisher, Ph.D. states, about both women and men, "Far from being desperately lonely, older people are the least likely to compromise and settle for less than a perfect relationship". (I want to know how she defines perfect.) And, she says, they are content with their singlehood. This same article, written by and about 50 year old Marion Winik, explores her life as a single woman, after two not so happily ever after marriages. And she loves it – the freedom to come and go as she pleases, to manage her own finances, and to make her own decisions. Winik was so pleased with her new found existence that she wrote a book celebrating the joys of the single life. And then, surprise, surprise, she met a man at a party. (Right now they are happily dating.)

Like Winik, I had created "a life worth living" - for myself and by myself (including of course, Sammy the dog and Callie the cat). Unlike Winik and some of my friends, I took the plunge again, knowing in my wisdom place and on a very deep level, that my fate was tied to his and that my growth and my happiness (and my ability to stretch) would blossom. I was right!

Disrupting Aging
Sixty Is Not the New Forty!

You know the expression "sixty is the new forty"? Well, I used to believe that - until I looked in the mirror and did not see my 40 year old face staring back at me – and I remembered how my hips used to move and my knees used to bend. And... I remembered that life wasn't all that great when I was younger, feeling lost at thirty, and at forty still grappling with "what do I want to be when I grow up". There are and were some realities of life that busted that myth right open!

I turned 68 in March and have been a proud, card-carrying member of AARP for a long time. Like I used to devour Cosmopolitan Magazine when I was young, I now read the AARP magazines and newsletters cover to cover. In the February/ March editions of both, there was an article and an interview by Jo Ann Jenkins, the CEO of AARP, about her new book "Disrupt Aging". She wants us to change the conversation about what it means to get older. One of the definitions of disrupt, she says, is to challenge - and in this case to challenge the aging process. Sixty is not the new forty, she says. But it is the new sixty! And therefore, seventy is the new seventy and so forth. We're living longer. We're healthier. And we're working longer into what Jenkins calls an extended middle age. Some of us have to – some of us want to.

Jenkins reminds us that years ago we didn't think about twenty plus years of living after retirement. Life expectancy was 67 and we would draw social security at 65. Here are three more stats from Jenkins that blew my mind: The fastest growing age group is now 85 and up. The one hundred plus age group is rapidly growing. And the fifty plus segment of the population generates $7 trillion in economic activity annually. Wow!

One important thing I've learned because of my continuing education as a psychotherapist is the impact that our self-talk, positive or negative, has on our health and well-being. Simply, if we talk to ourselves in negative ways, we'll believe those negative messages. We create negative neuro-pathways in the brain. (I'm too old to start a business or not smart enough to go back to school.) And conversely, we can create positive neuro-pathways and we will believe those positive messages. (I can do this! Yes, I can change careers!) We're more powerful than we think. We just don't know it. But it's challenging to muster the beliefs about a happy, healthy, productive life when we're absorbing so much negativity about aging from the culture at large. Just turn on a television and see how we are depicted!

Jenkins recounts her 50th birthday party and the messages on the cards from family and friends. "Over the hill... old geezer... young geezer... you're not losing it... you're how old?!" Just go to the card department of a local drug store and you'll experience what Jenkins felt. Angry! "I'm not over the hill", she said to herself, "I'm at the top of the mountain." She was 54 when she left her job as CEO of the Library of Congress to begin her tenure with AARP. I was 43 when I entered graduate school and 60 when I started my private practice.

My father retired when he was 60, after years of watching his dress manufacturing business decline, and then fail. The garment industry was in flux, first moving south where labor and material costs were less expensive, and then overseas. I remember him telling me that he never liked it. He hated going into the factory. Yet, day after day, for his family, he did. I learned important lessons from my father about giving myself permission to find what I love to do and about a strong work ethic. Hence I'm still working and doing what I love. After he and my mother settled in Florida, surprise, surprise, he got bored, very bored, and found two part-time jobs which he went to, on and off, until he died at age 80.

I don't know what retirement will look like for me. Will there even be a retirement? Maybe I'll be like Jo Ann Jenkins – and my dad – disrupting aging.

Conclusion

And in the end...
Some Final Thoughts

"For better and for worse" ... it was my husband who urged me to compile my *Jill* articles into this book. He believed that this collection of guidance, teachings, musings, research data, and self-disclosures would be of great value to all women—women who have struggled with their bodies and women who have not.

He also felt that it would be a great project for me—a way of looking at my own growth and transformation, as well as the evolutionary process of my programs.

He was right! I'm glad he nudged me! Thank you, Husband.

And thank you to my many clients over the years who have trusted me with your truths and your traumas. You are beyond courageous. You are my heroes!

I hope, dear Reader, that you have been both entertained and enlightened by this collection. I hope that you will hear my voice in your head and STOP when you think about a diet or an extreme exercise program or some kind of body reshaping surgery.

I hope I have helped you to see that we do, indeed, need a culture shift and that each of us can do our part in making that happen.

Let me hear your thoughts, please! You can reach me at ileneleshinsky@gmail.com and learn more about Find Body Freedom at www.findbodyfreedom.com.

www.ingramcontent.com/pod-product-compliance
Lightning Source LLC
Chambersburg PA
CBHW050909160426
43194CB00011B/2335